The Schools of Sampford Peverell
Two Centuries of Education

*by Carole Bond, Christopher Chesney,
Christine Mason, Jacky McKechnie, Jenny Parsons,
Peter Bowers and Vivienne Heeley*

A Sampford Peverell Society publication

Previous publications by the Sampford Peverell Society

A Village Childhood, *Denis Cluett, edited by Sampford Peverell Society, and published by Charles Scott-Fox, 2007*

Sampford Peverell: The Village, Church, Chapels and Rectories, *Editor and publisher Charles Scott-Fox, 2007*

Printed by Hedgerow Print Ltd

Published by the Sampford Peverell Society 2015

Copyright © Sampford Peverell Society

ISBN: 978-0-9933171-0-1

Contents

Introduction and Acknowledgements		i
Foreword		ii
Editor's Note		iii
Chapter I:	The Beginnings of Education in Sampford Peverell	1
Chapter II:	The National School 1874 – 1902	25
Chapter III:	East Devon County School 1863 – 1907	37
Chapter IV:	The Church of England School 1902– 1944	53
Chapter V:	The Church of England Primary School 1944 - 2000	77
Chapter VI:	Other Schools	95
Chapter VII:	2000 onwards	99
Appendix 1:	Sources	102
Appendix 2:	Head Teachers	104
Appendix 3:	Standards of Education	105
Appendix 4:	Attendance at the National School before 1900	107
Appendix 5:	Number of pupils at the Church of England School 1873- 2000	108
Appendix 6:	Punishment Book for the Church of England School 1911-1984	109
Index:	Index of Names	110

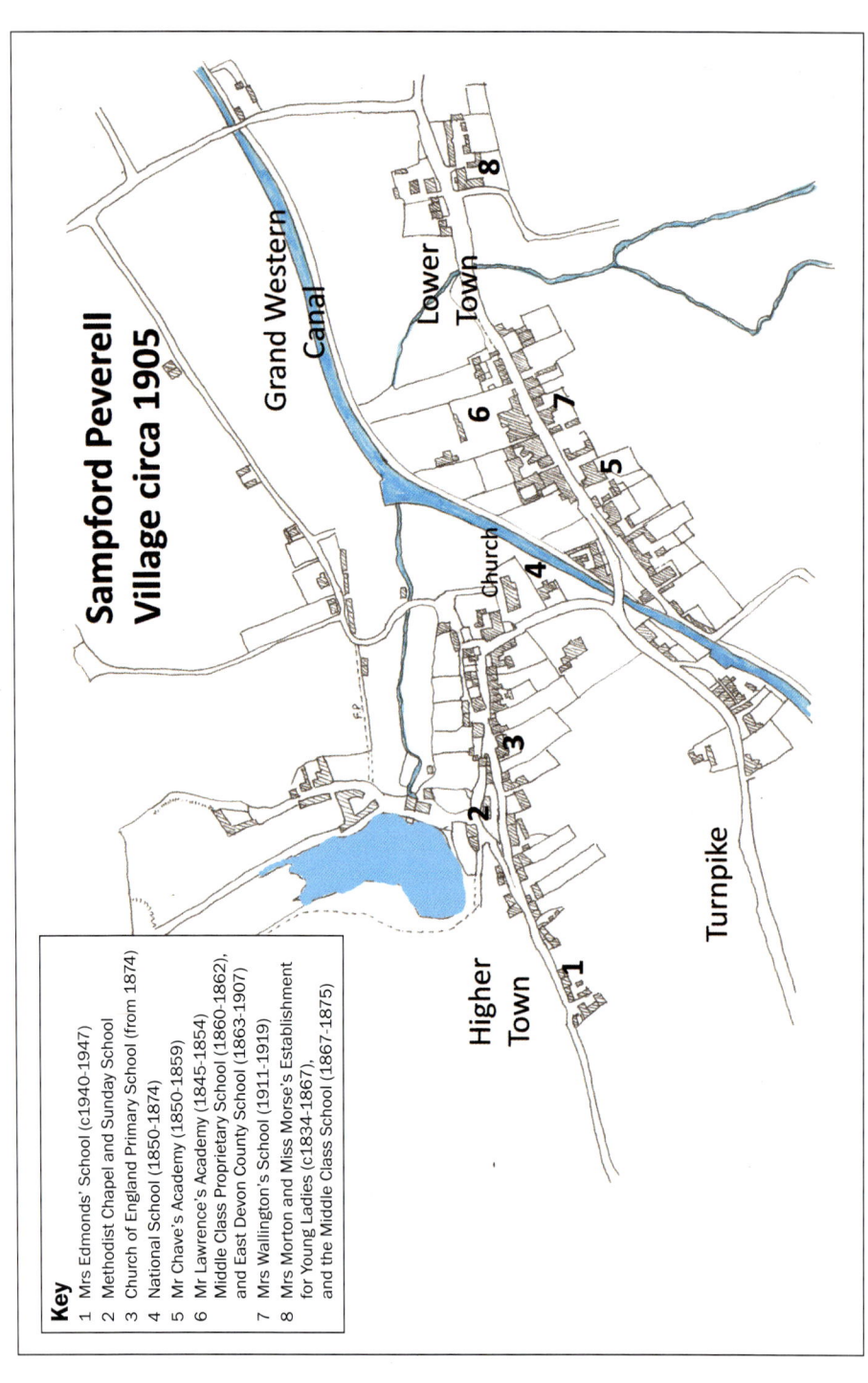

Introduction

This book, being the third by the Sampford Peverell Society, continues with our aim of researching the many aspects of the heritage of this parish. The research has been carried out by a team of volunteers, who then went on to write up their chosen chapters. The various drafts were then subjected to scrutiny by the whole team and finally the appointed editor brought the entire work together.

At the outset we had intended to include a chapter about the St Boniface Boys' Home, at one time situated in the village, but for a number of reasons it was subsequently decided that it would be better to cover this in a separate publication at a later date.

The team members for this book were: Carole Bond, Christopher Chesney (editor), Christine Mason, Jacky McKechnie, Jenny Parsons, Peter Bowers and Vivienne Heeley. I would especially like to express my thanks to my fellow team-members for all their hard work, patience and dedication, which has resulted in so much of the forgotten past of this fascinating village being re-discovered.

Acknowledgements

Whilst it is not possible to mention everyone who helped in some way with this work, the team members would particularly like to record their thanks to the Governors of Sampford Peverell Primary School for their permission to borrow, and make extracts from, the School Log Books and Punishment Book. Our thanks are also due to the staff of the Devon Records Office and Tiverton Museum of Mid-Devon Life for all their help and co-operation.

The names of those who kindly provided their reminiscences are shown in the text, whereas photographs are from a variety of sources: the School's own archive; the authors; Tiverton Museum of Mid-Devon Life; Helen Cowan, John Maclurcan (the Australian great-great-great grandson of Anthony Boulton), Kenneth Bass and Michael Rumsey; and the postcard collections of Jenny Holley, Bridget Bernhardt and Roger Greenwood. Where known, the name of the photographer is shown below the image. Michael Rumsey made suggestions on the draft text and contributed the Foreword. Allan Weller carefully proof-read the text, and provided advice on it. Finally, Christine Butler put the whole work together ready for printing.

Peter Bowers
Chairman Sampford Peverell Society 2015

Foreword

By Michael Rumsey, Head Teacher 1985 to 2000

It gives me great pleasure to write the foreword for this most excellent of publications which examines education in Sampford Peverell in detail. Having read the School Log books which started in 1872, I found them all quite fascinating. During my sixteen years as Head I had the pleasure of meeting quite a number of former pupils, some of whom had been residents at the St Boniface Home for Boys. The oldest of these visitors had arrived from Plymouth in 1910 and was resident at the Home until the outbreak of the First World War. His memory of how things were in those days was superb and when I showed him the Punishment Book, which started in 1911, he was fascinated to find his own name and recalled not only the punishment but the so-called crime which caused the caning!

The numbers 'on roll' in my time rose from seventy-two pupils to the highest post war figure of 125 children, owing to an influx of travellers' children. Space was very tight and we were relieved when numbers returned to the average of 110 to 115.

Education in Sampford Peverell Church of England Controlled Primary School in the 21st Century is vastly different from that in the previous two centuries and the reader of this book will enjoy the depth of detail that the writers have achieved in these pages. May I take this opportunity of thanking all those who have contributed to this publication and I sincerely hope that excellent education will continue in the village for generations to come.

Michael Rumsey
February 2013

Editor's Note

As editor, it has been my pleasurable task to co-ordinate the written work of the team. Each chapter was written by one or two members of the team, and so far as possible the 'voices' in each chapter are those of the respective authors. We also adopted a policy of adding information which we felt would be interesting, or shed further light upon subjects which may be remote to younger readers, by means of footnotes.

Many of the monetary amounts given in this history are in the pre-decimal £ s d format, one which will be unfamiliar to anyone born after 1972. These were the antique symbols for 'pounds, shillings and pence': there were 12 pennies to a shilling and twenty shillings to a pound. Thus a figure such as '£3 12s 11d' should be read as 'three pounds, twelve shillings and elevenpence. When just shillings and pennies were involved, then the notation for, say two shillings and sixpence, would be written as 2/6d. To further complicate matters, the penny could be divided into two or four portions, known respectively as half-pennies (pronounced ha'pennies) or farthings. To multiply, say £3 12s 11½d by 17, made small boys and girls concentrate very hard indeed. In addition to £ s d, the text also includes the terms guinea and guineas. Originally the name of an English gold coin, it was in Victorian times represented by the sum of £1 1s 0d. The term is used even now in some circumstances, such as auction sales, being equal to £1.05.

The present-day values of sums of money found in the records are given, where it was thought to be helpful. Such information was derived from the web site by Samuel Williamson at http://www.measuringworth.com/ukcompare/relativevalue.php.

Similarly, the pre-metric measurements of length were the inch, foot and yard. The notation for 'inches' was the inverted commas sign thus: 6''. That for the foot was a single inverted comma thus: 22'. The simpler notation is chiefly used in the text.

When quoting from our sources, every effort has been made to be accurate; however, if we have committed any blunders, then we alone are responsible.

Dr Christopher Chesney
2015

Sampford Peverell Church of England Primary School, 2015 *Photo: Peter Bowers*

Chapter I

The Beginnings of Education in Sampford Peverell

Whether you loved school or hated it, the education you received is responsible for you being able to read this book and to ensure you paid the correct money for it or received the right amount of change when you bought it. We take education for granted and give little thought to the fact that for centuries only the sons of the wealthy were considered worthy of benefitting from knowledge imparted by monks and other scholars. Girls of all classes were limited to domestic skills on the whole.

Two hundred years ago the aristocracy and the nouveaux riches preferred to keep their workforce ignorant and in their place – at the bottom of the social heap. However, there have always been the enlightened few who have battled against the odds to encourage the spread of education, thus allowing the general populace the chance to better themselves.

This book tells the story of how education evolved not in one of the country's great seats of learning, nor in a wealthy market town with endowed schools, but in the rural Devon village of Sampford Peverell. With much of Devon, and indeed the rest of the country, having had rural roots, parallels will be found between the development of education in this small parish and elsewhere throughout the land.

In the millennium up to the 17th century attempts to instigate education throughout the kingdom had experienced a bumpy ride, even for the wealthy. Not until the 1600s do we see the start of the steady, but by no means easy, movement towards the present system which offers education to everyone regardless of wealth, gender, or religious persuasion.

We know that whilst sons of the more wealthy inhabitants had been educated privately at home, the origins of education in schools in Sampford Peverell are poorly recorded. The Parish Records contain no reference to a school until 1844, when a Vestry Minute mentions that a meeting was to take place in the Parish School Room. There are, however, a few other sources that point towards an earlier date for the commencement of education. There are schools mentioned in the 1841 census of the Parish, this being the first for which personal details were recorded. This showed that Salome Morse and Jane Morton ran a ladies' boarding school at Turberfield House (see page 3); a young gentleman, Edwin Druller, who lived with his wife in Higher Town, described his occupation as Schoolmaster; and a lady named Susannah Knight who appeared to be a lodger in Higher Town, described her occupation as Schoolmistress. Mr Druller owned several properties, and it would seem probable that he ran a boys' day school in one of them, perhaps with Susannah Knight running a girls' day school either in the same premises or another nearby. The only surviving references to the schools in existence before this time are to be found in diocesan records, parliamentary records and newspapers.

The earliest surviving reference to a school in the Parish comes from questions and replies to the Episcopal Visitations in 1821[1]. The question for the Parish clergyman to answer was 'What Provision is there for the Instruction of Youth in Religion either by public or private Teaching?' The Revd Simon Pidsley replied 'There are two small Day Schools'. No further information was provided, so we cannot say where they were situated, or by whom they were run. However, records for Sampford Peverell's Methodist Chapel show that Samuel Jennings, who licensed his own house as a Meeting House in 1807, was a Schoolmaster, and Thomas Langford Pannell, one of the Chapel's Trustees in 1820, also gave his occupation as 'Schoolmaster'. One can conjecture that one of the two schools mentioned in the Episcopal Visitation was run by, and for, the Methodists.

Another source of information from this period is the 'Parliamentary Returns' for 1833, which paint a similar picture. These tell us that there were two schools, one with fifty pupils and the other with eighteen, both supported by parents except for twenty pupils whose fees were paid out of voluntary contributions.

Early newspaper articles and advertisements point to the Methodists as having led the way in the provision of schooling in the village. A newspaper for Methodists called 'The Watchman' carried an advertisement on 30 December 1835 - the first year of publication of this, the first newspaper for Methodists - for a 'Ladies' Establishment' run by Mrs Morton and Miss Morse, implying that the school was already in operation. This is probably one of the two schools recorded in the Parliamentary Returns two years earlier. In the Western Times of 9 November 1839 an article, reporting on the Centenary of Methodism, recorded the existence of a Methodist Sunday School in Sampford Peverell. It also mentioned that, 'until within a few years past, ...no religious instruction was afforded to the poor children of the establishment [i.e. the Church of England]'.

Furthermore, it alluded to the example set by the Methodists which had eventually led to the Rector supporting a free day school for the poor children of the Anglican

---

[1] At this time, Canon Law required Bishops to tour their dioceses every three years. Prior to each visitation, the Bishops sent questionnaires to Parish Clergy for them to complete, and some of these records have survived.

Church. A further example came in 1846 when another Methodist, Samuel Lawrence, placed advertisements in both The Watchman and the Western Times to attract boys for his 'Classical and Commercial Academy'.

To summarise, it would seem that the schools which were started in the early part of the 19th century were small, privately-run, and fee-paying (there being no record of any endowed schools or charitable ones). Some, if not all, were led by Methodists. They were not subject to any regulation and no other records are thought to have survived to illuminate them. Consequently, no more is known about them, and it is not until the foundation of the school for young ladies at Turberfield House that our account can begin.

Turberfield House – school for young ladies

Turberfield House in Lower Town dates from the 15th or 16th century. Originally a working farmhouse, it was occupied by a young surgeon by the name of William Farrant Merson, probably from the time of his marriage to Maria Morse (a farmer's daughter from Ashbrittle) on 24 December 1827, until about 1836. In 1833 they had one daughter, Maria, but her mother died within a few months and was buried in Sampford Peverell on 21 August 1834. Four years later, in 1838, William married Elizabeth Chave and went on to have a second family. In the 1841 census the address of William and Elizabeth was Lower Town and in the Tithe Apportionment of 1844 they were recorded as living in Chains Road, on Lower Town.

Turberfield House   *Photo: Peter Bowers*

Maria Merson senior had three sisters, Ann, Salome and Jane, and in the late 1820s the youngest, Jane, then in her late teens or early twenties, sailed to Canada, probably to be a teacher to immigrant families. Within a few years Jane, aged 25, met and married David Morton, also 25. He was a grocer, and the two married at St James Methodist Church, Montreal on 16 May 1831. The couple had two daughters, Amelia, born 1 March 1832 and Jane born 5 April 1834.

July 1834 saw the second, almost world-wide, pandemic of cholera (an acute and frequently fatal bacterial infection of the small intestine) hit Canada. Thought to be introduced to Quebec by infected Irish immigrants, 2509 people died between July and October 1834. Sadly one of the victims was David Morton at the early age of 28. Records show that he was buried in Montreal on 27 July 1834, only three months after the birth of his second daughter. Coincidentally Maria, Jane's eldest sister, was buried in Sampford Peverell just one month later.

Perhaps a combination of factors, namely her young husband's death from cholera; fearing for the safety of her daughters, and the death of her sister (leaving baby Maria motherless), caused Jane to abandon her life in the New World and come home to Devon.

Salome was, by this time, 32 and was still unmarried so she, perhaps, volunteered to care for the baby while Dr Merson was busy with his career. There is evidence of the closeness of the relationship between Salome and her niece on Maria's headstone in Sampford Peverell Churchyard on which Salome is referred to as being 'Buried near this spot. Dear aunt of Maria'.

During their tenure, Mrs Morton and Miss Morse advertised their school only in Methodist newspapers and not (as far as has been ascertained) in any others. The first such advertisement appeared in The Watchman in 1835, and it implied that the 'seminary' was already in operation. Further evidence of the sisters' commitment to the Methodist cause came in 1839, when their generous donations to the

> **LADIES' ESTABLISHMENT, SAMPFORD PEVERELL, NEAR TIVERTON, DEVON.**
> MRS. MORTON and Miss MORSE respectfully announce to their numerous Friends, that the duties of their SCHOOL will be resumed on the 18th of January.
> With feelings of liveliest gratitude, Mrs. and Miss M. retrospect the liberal encouragement and support which they have received for a series of years, and hope to merit a continuance of those favours by sedulous attention to the domestic comfort, health, moral and intellectual improvement, of those instructed to their care.
> The house is commodious, and pleasantly situated in an exceedingly healthy neighbourhood. Terms: - Board, with instruction in English, Composition, Astronomy, Geography with Globes, general Literature, Writing, Arithmetic, &c., 20 guineas per annum. Washing, 2 guineas.
> Music, French, and Drawing, 4 guineas each. Inlaying, Japanning, transparent Scene-painting, Painting on Glass, Velvet &c. on the usual terms.
> References given, on application, to the Friends of those Young Ladies who have been educated in the above Seminary.

The Watchman, 30 December 1835

Methodist Centenary Appeal Fund were recorded in the same organ. The Western Times of 9 November 1839, reporting on the celebration of the Centenary of Methodism in Sampford Peverell, mentioned the hospitality of Miss Morse. At her house (i.e. Turberfield House) she provided a roast beef and plum pudding dinner to members of the Methodist Sunday School, consisting of 157 children and nearly 50 families besides. One can only imagine that all the young ladies of the seminary were pressed into helping out at the event!

The 1841 census shows Jane to be a widow and living in Turberfield House, the property that was now leased to Salome. By this time Jane's daughters were aged 7 and 9, and the boarding school was well under way. The census shows there were twenty one girls aged between 8 and 15, and two 9 year old boys, brothers of two of the girl pupils, being educated there. On census night the record shows that three servants and a 15 year old School Assistant, Sarah Mainwaring, were also in residence. Despite having seven bedrooms the accommodation must have been 'cosy' to say the least, unless some of the numerous outbuildings were pressed into use.

The reason for Jane and her eldest sister, Salome, taking over Turberfield House is open to speculation, but it would seem reasonable to suppose that, if Jane had been engaged in an educational position in Canada and now had no visible means of supporting herself and her two little daughters, then perhaps an arrangement was reached whereby she joined her sister in running the boarding school, thus ensuring that the women could support themselves and all three girls.

Education appears to have become fashionable for the Morse family because, according to the 1841 and 1851 censuses, a first cousin of the sisters, James Morse, was running a boy's school in Yeovil. He, however, died in 1857 at the age of 54, and so his school was forced to close.

The 1851 census shows that Dr William Farrant Merson was a visitor at Turberfield House as a non-practising physician. He was 46 so it is unlikely he was retired, but rather that he had gone to visit his daughter, Maria. One is left to wonder why Dr Merson and his second wife, Elizabeth, did not take 4 year old Maria into their own home when they married in 1837. Was it a case of the new wife not wanting to take on another woman's child or was it simply the fact that Maria was settled with her aunts?

According to the 1851 census Amelia Morton had become a Schoolmistress along with her mother and her aunt, and there were nineteen girls between the ages of 9 and 18 boarding at Turberfield House. The census also shows that the school had attracted pupils born in places as diverse as Jamaica, Guernsey and Malta, as well as locally. A Governess, Sophia Keene aged 24, and Louise Horne, a 23 year old teacher of German born in Berlin, and three servants were also employed by the Morse/Morton family.

A further ten years on, in 1861, Salome had died (buried in 1854) but Jane and her daughter were still in business, although the Land Tax Return shows that Mrs Morton now 'shared' the property with a Mr Payne, and had two more nieces at the school, Amelia Morse (born 1845 in Ashbrittle) aged 16, and 14 year old Ann Morse (born 1847 in Skilgate). Two advertisements in The Watchman, both from 1859, show that pupils came from all parts of Great Britain and the Colonies, although 'Africans of colour are not admitted'.

MRS. MORTON'S Establishment for Young Ladies, Sampford Peverell, near Tiverton Junction, Devon, will re-open (D.V.) July 20.
Terms moderate for Board, Music, Singing, Drawing, the modern languages, every branch of a liberal education, including plain and ornamental needle-work.
The object of the Proprietress is to blend the happiness of home with the order and occupation needful to the attainment of a polite and useful education, to watch over the health of the pupils, and the religious culture of the mind.
Any parents who may entrust a child to Mrs. Morton's care can have the highest references to the friends of those she has had the pleasure of educating, both in Great Britain and the Colonies.

The Watchman, 22 June 1859

SAMPFORD PEVERELL
Near Tiverton Junction, Devon.
The Duties of Mrs. NORTON'S *[sic]* Establishment for Young Ladies will be RESUMED D.V. JANUARY 10th 1860.
The patronage which has bestowed and the success which has attended Mrs. Norton's system of tuition form for the parents a guarantee for the improvement and happiness of their children.
The course of education comprises music, singing, drawing, the modern languages, every branch of useful study plain and ornamental needle work.
Terms, moderate, forwarded on application; also references if desired to the parents of pupils in Great Britain and the colonies.
At the request of numerous friends Africans of colour are not admitted.

The Western Times, 31 December 1859

Six years later, in 1867, after many years of running the school, Jane Morton died and it was taken over by Mr James and Mrs Ann Hewett, formerly farmers at Middle Pitt, Sampford Peverell, according to the 1861 census.

Mrs Hewett lost no time in advertising in the Western Times newspaper, even before she had taken up residence, and in June 1867 the following advertisement appeared:

TURBERFIELD HOUSE, SAMPFORD PEVERELL – DEVON.
MRS. JAMES HEWETT begs to inform her friends that having taken the above house and premises, in which a School for Young Ladies has been successfully carried on for the last forty years, and having engaged an accomplished Lady as GOVERNESS, she is desirous of receiving a few YOUNG LADIES to be educated with her own children.
Her Pupils will be treated in every respect as her own family and will be thoroughly instructed in all the usual branches of a sound English education. The House is commodious, healthily situated, within a convenient distance from the railway station, and every attention will be paid to the comfort of those who may be entrusted to her care.
Further particulars on application. Dated Pitt Farm, Tiverton. June, 1867.

The Western Times, 28 June 1867

The school became the 'Middle Class School', in order to appeal to the English middle class, and the Hewetts advertised the fact that a great many alterations and improvements had been made to the establishment, which would offer the comforts of home, and girls would 'receive a thoroughly good liberal and practical education.' She engaged the services of a Governess, Louisa Killingley, aged 26, 'who has for several years proved herself one of the most successful teachers living.' Half-yearly examinations were to be carried out by 'Clergymen and Gentlemen', and Mr Robert Clouting, Head Master of the East Devon County School (See Chapter III), was happy to give Miss Killingley a good reference.

In 1868 the property was split into two. The 'School, Garden and Orchard' were in the occupation of Mr & Mrs Hewett, while Thomas Graves occupied "Turberfield". On 22 July 1870 James Hewett died and the following month Ann auctioned off his horse, cattle, cider press and other various lots. In view of the fact that James' Will records his assets as being 'less than £800', could the Hewetts have over-stretched themselves with all the alterations and improvements?

A year later the census indicates that Ann Hewett, her four children, three servants, the Governess and five boarding pupils were living at The Middle Class School, but in August 1875 the whole property was put up for sale by auction.

The death knell for Sampford Peverell's long-standing school for young ladies had rung, and the 1876 Land Tax Return shows Ann Hewett living in the House and Orchard (no mention of a school), while Turberfield was occupied by the new property owner, Mr W F Pedlar.

Mr Lawrence's Classical and Commercial Academy

This Academy was set up by Samuel Lawrence in about 1845, and was situated in a large property in Lower Town. These premises had previously been occupied by John Richard Chave, who moved to Bampton in 1845.

Born in Bristol in about 1813, Samuel Lawrence was still living there with his mother, sisters and others when the 1841 census was taken. His occupation was recorded as 'Minister'. In the following year, an announcement appeared in the Methodist newspaper 'The Watchman' (dated 13 July 1842), in which it was stated that Mr Samuel Lawrence of Kingsholm Academy, Gloucester had married Mary Taylor Chave, only daughter of the late Mr John Chave of Sampford Peverell, Devon. From this, we can infer that Samuel Lawrence's ministry was in the Methodist Church and that he had taken up a position at Kingsholm Academy only a year or so before he married. Mary Taylor Chave was the sister of John Richard Chave, whose story follows on page 10.

Mr Lawrence's Academy was in the building on the right of this photograph (seen here circa 1900)

In 1845, premises suitable for running a school in Sampford Peverell became vacant. This was part of the former tannery site, which John Richard Chave had been forced to vacate owing to his mounting debts. Perhaps persuaded by his wife (who may have been keen to return to Sampford Peverell to be near her family), Samuel Lawrence took over the detached house, together with a stable, walled garden and playground, and established his own "Classical and Commercial Academy" there. Initially, he advertised in the Western Times for boarders at sixteen guineas per annum, and day scholars at three guineas, noting that the premises were 'large and airy'.

Indeed they were large, because the 1851 census shows that there were twenty-two boys boarded there, aged between 7 and 17 years. Of these, eight were born in Devon, six in Somerset, four in the West Indies, one in the East Indies, one in Wales and two in London. The accommodation also housed Mr Lawrence's family (wife and five children aged under 7), one 19 year old teacher who had been born in the West Indies, a cook, a servant and a nursemaid.

> CLASSICAL AND COMMERCIAL ACADEMY, **CONDUCTED BY Mr. S. LAWRENCE,**
> *SAMPFORD PEVERELL, near Tiverton.*
> THE DUTIES of the above Establishment will be RESUMED On July 20th
> TERMS PER ANNUM
> Yearly Boarders .... 16 Guineas.
> Day Scholars .... 3 do.
> Sampford Peverell is delightfully situated on the Wellington and Tiverton Road, 9 miles from the former, and 5 miles from the latter place, and about 2½ miles from Tiverton Road Station.
> It is remarkable for its salubrity. The School Premises are large and airy.
>
> *The Western Times, 4 July 1846*

> **CLASSICAL, COMMERCIAL, and MATHEMATICAL ACADEMY,**
> (conducted by Mr. S. LAWRENCE,) Sampford-Peverell, near Tiverton. – In this Establishment, Young Gentlemen are carefully instructed in the usual branches of a liberal English Education, the Classics, and French. The system of instruction and Discipline includes the leading principles of the Glasgow system. Particular attention is paid to the morals, health, and domestic comfort of the Pupils. The domestic arrangements are under the care of Mrs. Lawrence. The pupils attend the Wesleyan Ministry. The situation of the School is remarkably healthy.
> The Duties will be resumed on the 19th of July.
> Numerous references to Ministers and Parents of Pupils can be given.
> Contiguous Station, - "Tiverton Junction", Bristol and Exeter Railway.

The Watchman, 23 June 1852.

In 1852, Samuel Lawrence was advertising for more pupils, but this time in The Watchman newspaper. In this advertisement, he made clear that 'The pupils attend the Wesleyan Ministry'. His method of teaching included the 'leading principles of the Glasgow system', a system initiated by David Stow, which aimed to cultivate not only the intellect, but also the affections and habits of the pupils. For reasons that we do not know, Mr Lawrence closed down the school and gave up his tenancy to the premises in 1854. They remained unoccupied for several years, but were re-advertised 'to let' in the Western Times on 31 December 1859, when they were described as 'lately occupied by Mr Samuel Lawrence, Schoolmaster'. Samuel Lawrence was to move to Weston super Mare, where he was schoolmaster at Osbourne House in 1861.

> # SAMPFORD PEVERELL, DEVON.
> ## *EXCELLENT FAMILY RESIDENCE.*
>
> To be LET, for such Term of Years as may be agreed on, or SOLD in Fee, with immediate possession, all that commodious and Genteel Detached
> DWELLING HOUSE AND PREMISES,
> *Situate in the Centre of Lower Town, Sampford Peverell,*
> With the Stable, Walled Garden, Yard, Playground, and all convenient Offices adjoining, lately occupied by Mr Samuel Lawrence, schoolmaster, &c.
> The House is well situated, and contains on the ground floor an entrance hall, dining, drawing, and breakfast rooms, with two kitchens, pump, scullery, and three arched cellars underground. There are six bedrooms on the first floor; and four other bedrooms may be added at a small expense.
> The above Premises are in substantial Repair, and are fit either for the immediate Residence of a large Family, or for occupation as a School, for which purpose the Premises are well adapted, and have been occupied for some years past.
> Mr. WILLIAM ADAMS, Sampford Peverell, will shew the Premises on application; and further particulars may be obtained at the Offices of Mr. R. T. HEAD, Solicitor, Bedford Circus, Exeter; or of
> Mr. WM. PARTRIDGE, Solicitor, Tiverton.   Tiverton, 13 July, 1854

Western Times, 22 July 1854

Mr Chave's Commercial and Mathematical Academy and Mrs Chave's Seminary for Young Ladies

John Richard Chave was born in 1810 into the family that was at the centre of the Sampford Ghost mystery. Around the time that he was baptised in October of that year, the story of the ghostly happenings and apparitions in the Chaves' house in Higher Town Sampford Peverell were being featured in newspapers all over the country. His father, John Chave, was also involved in the navvies' riot in Sampford Peverell in 1811, when about 300 navvies, engaged in building the new canal, caused mayhem in the village, because they had not been paid. The navvies picked on Mr Chave, who had no connection with their complaint, but was known to them on account of the Sampford Ghost story. The navvies followed him to his house, where he defended himself by shooting and fatally wounding one of them. At the subsequent inquest the death was determined to be 'justifiable homicide'. John Chave was at that time a huckster[2], running a shop from his home in Higher Town. He was from an extensive family of yeoman farmers in the nearby villages of Halberton, Burlescombe and in Sampford Peverell, but it would seem that both John Chave and his son John Richard chose to make their living by other means.

In 1841 the son, John Richard Chave, was involved in the lime trade. He owned a pebble rock quarry (from which lime could be extracted) situated off Whitnage Lane in Sampford Peverell, and known as Great Hill. In the 1841 census of Sampford Peverell he was living in Lower Town with his wife Eleanor, their two young children and four servants, and described his occupation as a lime burner. For a small household to have as many as four servants was very unusual: perhaps some were also involved in his business. It would seem that he was getting into financial difficulties, because in 1843 he conveyed all his estate and effects to four trustees, for the benefit of his creditors. In the following year, the entire quarry, lime kilns etc. were auctioned, presumably to satisfy his creditors.

The next we know of John Richard Chave is in 1845, by which time he had moved to Bampton with his family, and had commenced a new business as an auctioneer. There he rented a 'genteel family residence in Britain Street' (now 'Briton Street') which was clearly quite a substantial building. During their time in Bampton Eleanor gave birth to twin daughters, but there is no further mention of the auctioneering business. Perhaps it foundered. By 1850 the family, now consisting of Mr and Mrs Chave and their six children, had returned to Sampford Peverell and had set up a small day school in their home in Higher Town. Whilst John Richard Chave was the schoolmaster, Eleanor Chave worked as a milliner and dressmaker. The business, styled as a "Commercial and Mathematical Academy", started off well; indeed, he was advertising to take in young gentlemen as boarding pupils, with rates from twelve guineas (under 10s) to fifteen guineas (over 12s)[3]. There

---

[2] A 'huckster' was a vendor of small wares and knick-knacks.

was one stipulation: 'each young gentleman must be provided with a knife, fork, spoon and towels'!

Mr Chave advertised to take on twelve more young gentlemen in September 1853, but the Higher Town home may have been inadequate for further expansion. In the following year, at about the same time as his brother-in-law Samuel Lawrence gave up his school in Lower Town, J R Chave's Commercial and Mathematical Academy moved to 'Sheppard's Tenement', a large and modern house in Lower Town. Today, 'Sheppard's Tenement' is known as 'The Merriemeade', having become a public house in the 1960s. As part of this expansion, Mr John Bidgood was taken on as a teacher (although he also worked as an agent for Royal Farmers' Insurance Company), with Mr Chave remaining as the schoolmaster. By now, Mrs Chave was heavily involved in the running of the school, attending to the 'Domestic Department'. A governess had also been employed to educate a limited number of young ladies along with her own daughters. At its peak, there were twenty-five young gentlemen

> **AT CHAVE'S** *COMMERCIAL AND MATHEMATICAL ACADEMY,* SAMPFORD PEVERELL THERE are arrangements made for the reception of TWELVE PUPILS.
> The domestic comforts, strict attention to duties, Introduction to penmanship, commercial correspondence, healthiness of the locality, moderate charges &c., are unrivalled.
> Pupils fitted for any station in the commercial world.
> Terms and testimonials forwarded on application.

Exeter & Plymouth Gazette, 17 September 1853

Rear view of the Merriemeade in 1875, after refurbishment by new owners   Courtesy of Susan Bailey

[3] These fees are presumed to be per annum, although are never stated as such. Fifteen guineas equates to about £1,200 today using the retail price index as a comparator. Fees for Blundell's School, Tiverton in 2015 were up to £30,525 for a boarder.

boarding, together with a few day pupils. Terms had been increased, ranging from seventeen to nineteen guineas, ('including laundress') for boarders, and from three to four guineas for day scholars. There were additional charges for lessons in dancing, French, drawing, 'Use of the Globes', and an extra guinea for a single bed.

The boys were taught a wide range of subjects: reading, writing, arithmetic, English grammar, book-keeping (by single and double entry), geography, history, geometry and mensuration (deriving the length, area or volume of something by measurement and calculation). The girls, on the other hand, were taught English, French, music and drawing.

In an advertisement for the Academy from 1858, Mr Chave explained his principles: 'Corporeal [sic] punishment is avoided as much as possible, whilst every encouragement is given to diligent and deserving pupils by appropriate rewards; and nothing is omitted in providing

---

CHAVE'S WELL ESTABLISHED COMMERCIAL ACADEMY, SAMPFORD PEVERELL, DEVON.
REPLETE with every convenience for the comforts of his Pupils, will be RE-OPENED for the reception on MONDAY, The 14th day of January next.
Terms Moderate and Fare of the Best.
Most respectable reference given on request.
A spacious well sheltered Play Ground containing an extensive covered Shed.   26th Dec. 1855.

A select and limited number of **YOUNG LADIES** received by Mrs.CHAVE, to Educate with her daughters, under accomplished Governesses
Terms Moderate and Fare of the Best.
The Duties will be RESUMED ON MONDAY, JANUARY 14.

A GOVERNESS wanted to teach, English, French, Music,and Drawing.
Applicants to state Terms and References. 26th Dec., 1855

Western Times, 29 December 1855

SHEPHERD'S HOUSE ACADEMY.
SAMPFORD PEVERELL.
JOHN RICHARD CHAVE, in returning thanks for the liberal support he has already received, begs to make known the extensive alterations for the convenience of his establishment and the comfort of his pupils are now complete.
TERMS, INCLUDING LAUNDRESS: -
                                                    Per annum.
Above 12 years of age ... ...   19 Guineas
Under "   "   " "   ... ...   17 Guineas
                    EXTRAS: —
Latin, French, and Drawing ... ... £3 3s. each.
Use of the Globes   ... ... £2 2s.   "
Vacancies for 20 Pupils. Prospectuses forwarded on application. Extensive and well-sheltered play ground, with conveniences for recreation in wet weather.

MRS CHAVE'S SEMINARY.
Terms, including Laundress, 18 Guineas per annum.
A Governess Wanted to teach English, French, Drawing, Music and Singing. Applicants to state age, terms, and Reference.
May 22nd, 1856.

Exeter and Plymouth Gazette, 31 May 1856

their comfort, happiness and improvement.' A subsequent advertisement added another principle, of 'total abstinence.'

In December, at the end of term, there was a 'break-up' dance with festivities. This was also the occasion for prize-giving to the most proficient boys. At the break-up dance in December 1856, the boys danced a 'fashionable programme' under the tutelage of Mr Bidgood; the musically-talented governess sang, and the principal scholars recited several pieces.

Shepherd's Academy

The Academy was situated at Sheppard's, Lower Town, a building of three storeys and an underground cellar. Mr Chave named his academy after the property, but chose the conventional spelling 'Shepherd's'. It was substantially built, well-drained and ventilated, and modern by the standards of the day. Initially, Mr Chave was the tenant of this property, which was described as being 'double-fronted (North and South)', and had a walled garden, an orchard of about three quarters of an acre, and several outbuildings. He made several improvements to the premises, starting with an extensive shed to cover the playground in 1855, costing £100 in materials alone[4]. A purpose-built schoolroom was then added, funded by pupils' parents, which was completed in 1857. Having made these improvements, he purchased the reversion of the lease for £500, thus ensuring that he could continue to occupy the property when the lease terminated.

An inventory of the property's contents, drawn up in 1859 for their auction, provides considerable insight into the layout of the premises and of the furniture contained therein. The second floor of the building, a large open plan attic room, was the boys' dormitory. On the first floor were five bedrooms. Mr and Mrs Chave's room was on the west side of the south front, furnished with an American birch half-tester bed and several items of mahogany furniture. The East bedroom of the south front was probably for their children, containing four beds and a crib. Also on this floor were a nursery, the governess's bedroom, and the young ladies' bedroom with three beds.

On the ground floor were to be found the principal rooms of the house: the sitting room, which was well-furnished and clearly the province of the Chave family; the dining room, where the boys ate and carried out other activities such as washing, making tea and preparing meals; the young ladies' schoolroom, furnished with a writing-desk and piano; the young ladies' dining room; the 'best' kitchen, larder and scullery, and the servants' bedroom. (We deduce that there was more than

---

[4] This sum would today be about £7,900, using the rise in the retail price index since 1855.

one servant because, although the room contained only one bed, it had three chairs. It was common for servants to have to share a bed, but not one chair.)

The boys' schoolroom was well provided with text books and a large quantity of copy books (twenty-five dozen!). Teaching was not only from textbooks, but also by educational games and 'useful knowledge' games. The boys sat at long desks, on wooden forms (sufficient to accommodate forty pupils), presided over by the master and assistant master.

Demise of the Academy

Mr Chave's intention had been to turn his successful Academy into a proprietary school[5]. For this, he had the support of the local clergy: Revd Bere of Uplowman and Revd Ireland of Sampford Peverell. This ambition was thwarted, owing to Mr Chave having fallen into financial difficulties. Disaster had struck in July 1858 when a fire broke out in the outbuildings which spread to the school-room, causing much damage. The fire brigade from Tiverton, under Captain Hobbs, was called out and 'being indefatigable in their exertions, the flames were prevented extending to the dwelling house'. The report in the Exeter Flying Post on the 29th of July 1858 concludes 'We are glad to be able to state that Mr Chave is insured', and indeed £300 was paid out by the Insurance Company. Fortunately, the fire did not seriously affect the running of the establishment: two months later, Mr Chave was advertising vacancies at the Academy once more, it having been re-fitted after the fire. The Academy continued for another year, but then there was a very quick turn of events. Having advertised that the school would re-commence on 19 July 1859, only a month later preparations were being made to sell the entire contents and the freehold of the property.

The reason for the sudden change was Mr Chave's mounting debts. Not only did he owe money for the building of the playground shed, and had bought the reversion of the lease, but he had also embarked upon extending the premises by adding another house. This had cost about £300, although it was unfinished. He had mortgaged the property to local businessman Mr John Norrish, but had also taken loans from a Mr Hayward, who was the secretary of the Wellington Building Society. In July 1859 he assigned all his estate and effects to two trustees for the benefit of his creditors, because he had become hopelessly indebted and Mr Hayward refused to lend him any more.

On 18 and 19 August 1859, the entire contents of the property were sold at auction by a Mr Snell, to whom they had been mortgaged in 1857. The sale raised £111;

---

[5] Proprietary schools were schools owned by shareholders. Typically, proprietorship of a share entitled its holder to send or nominate a child to the school.

the items that realised the most were two pianos for £24 10s 0d. The freehold property was put up for auction on 8 September 1859, being advertised as suitable for a gentleman's residence or for 'an extensive proprietary establishment', but it did not sell at that time. In addition to the building that had been used when it functioned as the Academy there were 'some extensive buildings, nearly completed, which can be finished at a very small outlay, and will then form another spacious and commodious residence... The whole is so constructed as to form, if desired, one spacious residence which would contain twelve bedrooms'.

Mr Chave had now lost his livelihood, but remained in Sampford Peverell until July 1860 before taking up a new role. He took over Beadon's Academy in Gandy Street, Exeter, upon the death of Mr Beadon, and renamed it Chave's Commercial and Mathematical School. In addition to the tuition of young gentlemen, he also advertised evening classes for 'Parents and all persons occupied by day in business and desirous of improvement in General Accounts and Book-keeping'. Despite his best endeavours, and partly due to his illness, pupil numbers began to fall and the debts that he had left behind in Sampford Peverell were still unsettled. Finally, in January 1864, he petitioned to the Exeter Court of Bankruptcy, and was adjudged to be bankrupt. It was ascertained that he had total debts of £1130[6], with assets of just £48. After a full examination of his finances, the judge concluded that he had taken on more debts whilst already being insolvent, but that he had not had a fraudulent intent. He was granted a discharge after twelve months, and the protection of the Court.

But being a discharged bankrupt was not an end to Mr Chave's problems. He was fortunate enough to find employment with a Crediton spirit merchant, John Badcock at a salary of £60 per annum. However, after a few months, a dispute arose between them, which led to Mr Chave's immediate dismissal. Mr Chave had withheld some of the proceeds from the sale of Mr Badcock's goods because he had not been paid the second instalment of his salary. The case went to court in May 1865 and the judge agreed with Mr Badcock's decision to dismiss him. He ordered Mr Chave to return a small sum to Mr Badcock, and both sides had to pay their own costs.

After this setback, it appears that Mr Chave moved from Exeter back to Sampford Peverell (where his mother still lived), and took up a position of 'manure agent'. In June 1866 The Western Times reported a fatal accident. 'Mr Chave (manure agent) was driving home from Tiverton, and when near the Swan Inn at Halberton[7], the wheel of the gig came in contact with the kerb, causing the vehicle to upset.

---

[6] Today worth about £87,000, using the rise in the retail price index since 1864.

[7] The Swan Inn was in Higher Town, Halberton. It lost trade after the turn of the 19th century and in 1919 the owners Starkey, Knight & Ford Ltd. (Brewers), sold it to Halberton for use as a Memorial Village Hall (WW1). It still remains in Higher Town, now the High Street, as the Village Hall.

Mr Chave was thrown violently to the ground and sustained such severe injuries that he died on the following day.' He is buried in the churchyard of St John the Baptist Church, Sampford Peverell.

As for the former Academy, local farmers and tradesmen with an interest in keeping an educational establishment in the village stepped in to help. A school had opened again by the following year, probably retaining several of the day pupils, and initially operated under the name 'Sampford Peverell Middle Class Proprietary School'. The story is continued in Chapter III.

The National School (until 1874)

Established in 1811, the 'National Society for the Education of the Poor in the Principles of the Established Church' expanded rapidly, so that Anglican schools were set up in most parishes by the second half of the nineteenth century. In Sampford Peverell, the National School was first established in 1850 in the Old Rectory. The owners of this property, the Grand Western Canal Company, had acquired it by Act of Parliament in 1811 to facilitate the construction of the Canal through the Rectory's land. By way of recompense, the Canal Company was required to build a new Rectory but, owing to lack of funds, it did not manage to do so until 1841. Over this thirty year period, the Rector remained in residence at the Old Rectory, during which time little or no maintenance was carried out upon it. When the new rectory, currently known as Church House, was at last completed opposite the Old Rectory, the Rector duly moved in to the new building and the Old Rectory became vacant. By this time, the Old Rectory had fallen into a parlous state of repair and the Canal Company must have been eager to dispose of it.

The Poor Law Amendment Act of 1834 required parishes to make existing parish accommodation available for the use of schools. In 1834 and for some years after, Sampford Peverell did not (as far as we know) have such accommodation available, but it seems probable that the Rector, Revd Edward Pidsley, provided room for a school in the Old Rectory. The final sentence of a report in the Western Times of 9 November 1839 informs us that the Rector supported, chiefly by his own donation, a free school for the sons and daughters of the poor of the Church of England. When the Rector moved out of the Old Rectory to the new house in 1841, the school was able to remain in the dilapidated building. It seems likely that reference to the 'Parish School Room' in the Vestry minutes of 1844 was in fact a reference to one of the rooms in the Old Rectory, which was by then being used for the purpose of a school, but without any formal constitution.

The catalyst for putting 'education for all' in Sampford Peverell on a proper footing came in 1847, when the Revd Dr Anthony Boulton took over the position of Rector of the Parish. He had previously been the Under-Master at Blundell's School,

Tiverton, for a period of eighteen years until his retirement in 1845. There, he had been held in the highest regard, to the extent that he had been presented with an engraved silver salver and tankard, to the value of ninety guineas, at his retirement dinner.

In the year after his appointment as Rector, matters were put in hand to set up the Sampford Peverell National School. An application for funds was submitted to the Lords of the Committee of Council on Education by nine gentlemen of the Parish, with the Revd Dr Boulton to act as their Correspondent[8]. The application states these gentlemen were the chief promoters of a subscription towards the expense of building a school for eighty boys and sixty-six girls, being the children of the labouring, manufacturing and other poorer classes of the Parish, whose inhabitants were chiefly employed in agriculture. It goes on to say that there were no 'gentlemen of property' resident in the Parish who could be called upon to make a significant contribution towards the costs, and that the only landowner of any consequence was a dissenter[9] and 'therefore not disposed to give much towards establishing a Church School'.

Revd Dr Anthony Boulton, circa 1850. He died in 1854   Courtesy of John Maclurcan

Consequently, without a grant from the Lordships, a school could not be built.

The building to be used for the National School was the Old Rectory, which was 'in a very dilapidated state in the interior', but an architect had pronounced that it was structurally sound, and capable of bearing a slate roof in place of the thatched one. The costs were to be £100 for the purchase of the building and garden plus £165 for renovations and new roof. Although the existing lime and sand floors were considered adequate, the renovation plans did include warming the school with

---

[8] These were: Revd Dr Anthony Boulton, Richard Skinner (farmer), Henry Broom (maltster), John Beedell (farmer), James Hewett (farmer), Richard Penkivil (surgeon), Richard Shackell (butcher), John Surridge (yeoman) and William Payne (farmer).

[9] In this context, a dissenter was one who refused to accept the doctrine of the Church of England. In Sampford Peverell the dissenting Churches were Wesleyan Methodist and Bible Christian.

The Old Rectory, circa 1890, after it had ceased to be a school. The new owners, Mr and Mrs Burrough, sit outside.

'Arnotts thermometer stoves'[10]. Gutters and wooden spouts would be provided to the new slate roof, so that rainwater would be coursed through the privies into the canal. The application was successful in obtaining a grant of £100 from the Lords of the Committee of Council on Education, and a separate grant of £50 was obtained from the National Society. The remaining £84 17s 0d was raised from private subscriptions. By a deed dated 25 September 1850, the building was granted to the minister and churchwardens 'Upon trust for a school for the labouring, manufacturing and other poorer classes in the parish and a residence for the teacher or teachers of the said school, and for no other use; such school always to be in union with and conducted in accordance with the principles of the National Society.' The deed also required the minister to have superintendence of the religious and moral instruction of the scholars, and allowed for a Sunday School to be run on the premises.

---

[10] Dr Neil Arnott (1788–1874), physician and natural philosopher, was born at Arbroath, Scotland. About 1855, he gave up his practice, and turned his attention to scientific and sanitary matters, inventing a smokeless grate, known as 'Arnott's Stove'. For this he was awarded the Rumford medal of the Royal Society. At http://www.historyhome.co.uk/people/arnott.htm. Accessed November 2013

With the future of the premises secured, works took place to restore the building, which is commemorated in a plaque above the front door of the Old Rectory. These works, organised by the incumbent Rector, were later to be much criticised by Rector G W R Ireland, when he wrote 'It [*i.e. The Old Rectory*] was further spoilt by Dr Boulton, a former Rector, who lowered the central portion of the building thus destroying two or three bedrooms and the fine oak staircase.' However badly these works were carried out, the building was at least saved from ruin, and the original ground floor ceilings have remained intact. The two-storey north wing is believed to have become the master's residence, and a new external doorway was made to give direct access from the front garden. The single-storey hall would have been divided into separate sections for the boys' and girls' school-rooms.

Plaque above the main door of the Old Rectory
Photo: Peter Bowers

The Old Rectory today, with the second storey restored   Photo: Dixon Cowan

Mr John Vickary [*otherwise Vickery*] was the first master of the National School, and his wife Elizabeth the first mistress. Mr Vickary also held the position (from 1848 until his death in 1856) of Overseer and Vestry Clerk for the Parish, for which he received £15 pa. During the Vickarys' tenure, the number of children reportedly stood at seventy-five, and the school was 'supported by subscription and by payments from the children'. In the early years of the School, the subscriptions were paid annually by most of the small farmers, and the initial expectation was that between £15 and £20 would be raised in this way[11]. The 'payments of the children' were to be one penny a week, and two pence if taught to write ('the School Pence'[12]). Although these payments may appear small, in the context of the wages of agricultural labourers in the area at that time, they were significant. A male agricultural worker would receive seven or eight shillings a week, from which he had to pay for food, clothing, rent etc. for his family. This led to much hardship and extremely poor housing and diets, with many labourers simply not able to afford to send their children to school when they could be out earning to help support the household.

In 1864 there was an outbreak of Scarlet Fever (a streptococcal infection with fever and a scarlet rash) in the village, which resulted in the deaths of seventeen children under the age of 13. This was the worst incidence of child mortality since the smallpox epidemic of the 1740s, and must have had a devastating effect upon the inhabitants. It is possible that school attendance fell from this time, with parents being concerned about the spread of infection amongst children in a confined space.

The financial arrangements were to change when Mr William H Biddlecombe, who had been born in Salisbury, was appointed as schoolmaster and organist in March 1865, together with his wife Eliza (twenty-two years his junior)) as the schoolmistress. He had previously been in the same role at Uplyme, Devon, near Lyme Regis, for thirteen years, and presumably came with a good reference. Because the school refused to come under the then optional scheme for inspection, it did not qualify for any parliamentary funding and the salary had to be raised locally. The Vestry Committee agreed to pay a salary of £40 pa 'with the School Pence and the School House and Garden rent-free'. Unfortunately, his term of office proved to be fairly short-lived, because it was unanimously agreed by the Vestry Committee to give him notice that his services would not be required from March 1869. Perhaps it was poor teaching performance that led to his dismissal, because the next record of him is from Silverton parish in 1871, where he held the occupation not of 'schoolmaster and organist', but just of 'organist'.

---

[11] About £1,100 to £1,700 today.

[12] The 'School Pence' refers to the one or two pence a week paid by each pupil, a system that remained in place until 1891 when it was abolished by the 1891 Elementary Education Act.

A Vestry meeting was held on 22 September 1870 to consider the Government's Elementary Education Act passed in February of that year. This Act (also known as the Forster Act[13]) enabled elected School Boards to be set up to provide facilities for education, where this was lacking or deficient, for children aged 5 to 12 years inclusive, at public expense. Under the Act, ratepayers in a parish could petition the Board of Education for the provision of schooling to be investigated. Such an investigation compared the number of school places available with a theoretical number that could attend, based upon the population recorded in a census, to be conducted in 1871. The Vestry committee must have done a rough calculation, from which they deduced that the existing premises were undersized.

Six weeks later, at a subsequent Vestry meeting, Revd G W R Ireland (the Rector of the parish) offered the freehold title of some land on which the new school could be erected, and undertook to have the land conveyed to the Rector and Churchwardens or other trustees for use as a National School 'for ever'. He also undertook to carry out the architect's plans at his own cost, save for £200 which was to be guaranteed by the Parish and other subscribers. This was unanimously agreed by the meeting, and a plan was made to repay the Rector the £200 in the following year.

Why had the Rector decided to pay for the new school largely out of his own funds, rather than allow a School Board to be set up and provide one at public expense? Was it because he wanted to be remembered as a major benefactor not only to the Parish Church, which he had had restored at his own considerable expense in the previous decade, but also to the whole community? One could speculate that this was not his prime motive. Rather, he perhaps may have wanted to maintain control over the religious education in the School, along strictly Anglican lines. One of the requirements under the Act was that religious education in a Board School had to be non-denominational, and Revd Ireland would not have welcomed this. Sampford Peverell had a very well-supported Wesleyan Methodist Church and according to the 1851 Census of Religious Worship, more people attended Sunday services at the Methodist Chapel than at St John the Baptist Church[14]. With many of the rate-payers being Methodist, there was a strong possibility that they could petition the Board of Education for a Board School to be built, which would completely side-line the inadequately-sized National School.

The action taken by Revd Ireland was by no means unusual. In Devon (excluding Exeter and Plymouth) between 1871 and 1874 there were fifty-nine new National Schools and other Voluntary Schools built, compared with just seven Board

---

[13] The 1870 Act was drafted by William Forster, a Liberal MP.

[14] This was a one-off census carried out on the same day (Sunday 30 March) as the Population Census of that year, which required all places of worship in England, Wales and Scotland to submit reports of their attendances, sittings and other statistical information.

Schools. It seems that many other Anglican priests, whether financed by their own funds or by those of their wealthy parishioners, were taking the same measures. It was only from 1876 onwards that the number of new Board Schools built annually in Devon exceeded the number of new National Schools, presumably because fewer Anglican benefactors came forward.

During the period from 1871 to 1874 when the new school building was under construction, an official from the Education Department visited Sampford Peverell to establish whether a new school was required under the Act. His report confirmed that it was necessary, partly on account of the inadequate size of the existing premises, since he had calculated that some 120 pupils might attend. A file note also states: 'H.M.I. [*Her Majesty's Inspector*] reports most unfavourably of both the building and instruction'. However, the Education Department deemed the new building under construction to be more than adequate: the 45' by 22' room, with a separate classroom of 22' by 15', would accommodate 165 children. This equated to just eight square feet per pupil for the whole premises!

School Log Book entry for 6 July 1872

Over the three years from the departure of Mr Biddlecombe in 1869, there was a succession of masters, and the quality of education was very poor. It was in 1872 that the Revd Ireland decided to bring the school under 'Inspection for Grant', either purely for financial reasons (by doing so, the school would qualify for a maintenance grant of up to fifty per cent), or also with a view to raising standards. When a new master, William Lloyd, took up his duties in June 1872, he started making entries in a log book, a practice that was kept up until it ceased to be a statutory requirement in 2000. Here are some extracts from the comments he made after having been present for one week:

> 'There were only five children present on the re-opening morning, but during the week the number gradually increased to 17. I found the children extremely ignorant in all subjects.'... 'I find it a most difficult matter to understand them speak even the most simple sentences viz. to ascertain their names (it is too guttural)'... 'Writing – the holding of the pen properly not known'... 'Discipline - in the most wretched condition - children rush headlong into and out of school and speak of each other to me as "Dick and Jack". They are not stolid but seem like unbroken colts. It will take more time at present to get them into like order'.

Unfortunately, Mr Lloyd was not to last long: his last entry in the log book was on 23 August, just two months after he had commenced. The school was then closed for three months whilst another master was found: Mr Jonathan Job. He was an inexperienced teacher, with only a Provisional Certificate, and would have been paid a lower salary accordingly. Not surprisingly, his first impressions were also unfavourable 'There were twenty-six children present and I found, after examining them, that not one of them would be able to pass the 1st Standard'[15]. It was not until 5 March 1874 that the improvements made through teaching were acknowledged. On that day, the first report of Her Majesty's Inspector was received, and read as follows 'The school has passed a pretty fair examination, considering the former neglected state of the children. Arithmetic and Spelling require attention. Singing is fair, sewing moderately fair'.

Tailpiece

The beginnings of education in Sampford Peverell can be seen as being polarised between that provided for the children of poor agricultural labourers and that available to the offspring of rather wealthier tradesmen and farmers. For the latter, although separate schools for boys and girls had been present, they suffered from being entirely dependent upon the fortunes and desires of the owners, who were also the principal teachers. Consequently, when one closed for whatever reason, the education of the children was disrupted until they could be found a place at another suitable establishment.

For the labouring classes, the National School provided more likelihood of continuity, but generally a poor standard of education, often failing to provide even the basic level to which it aspired. Several masters had only a short tenure, the position seemingly attracting the less able or less qualified who were willing to accept the comparatively low remuneration offered. Consequently, attendance at the school was often very low, with the parents not considering the standard of education offered sufficiently worthwhile to withhold their children from more productive work, or simply not able to afford the payments due to their impoverished state.

The shortcomings in both educational systems were to be addressed in the years that followed, as will be seen in the next two chapters.

---

[15] See Appendix 3 for a description of all six Standards.

Aerial photo of the School, circa 1991, opened in 1874 and still in use.

Photo: Mervyn Garland

Chapter II

The National School 1874 – 1902

Chapter I has described the establishment in 1850 of the Sampford Peverell National School and the introduction of the important Elementary Education Act of 1870. On 1st June 1874, twenty four years after its establishment, there was what, in retrospect, seems a momentous occasion in the history of our village school: the opening of the new school building. It is recorded very simply and abruptly by the Master, Mr Jonathan Job, as 'commenced teaching in the new School Room.' As far as we know there was no banging of drums, flag waving, banner displays or any speeches, just an ordinary school day in the newly built school in Higher Town.

> June 1 Commenced teaching in the new School-room. Visited by the Rev. P. C. Rositer and received of him 12 new books for Standard IV, 4 dozen for Standard II, and 4 dozen for Standard I. Also received Reading Sheets for the Infants. Admitted 29 new scholars. Mrs Farr commenced teaching the infants. Gave the children some desk-drill.

School Log Book entry for 1 June 1874

The building, as far as we can ascertain, was one room with a large fireplace at each end. The new schoolroom measured 60' by 22' and was calculated to hold 165 children. It was divided into two, possibly by a curtain, with the small part 15' by 22'. On the opening of the new building Mrs Mary Farr was employed as the infant teacher, so it is likely that the smaller area was used as the infants' classroom. Twenty years later a new porch and cloakroom were added on the north side next to the road. In the Report from Her Majesty's Inspector of Schools (HMI), following his inspection of 1886, it was recommended that a gallery should be installed in the infants' class, but there is no record of this having been carried out.

The Rector of the Parish, the Revd G W R Ireland, who had funded the new school (see Chapter I), must have decided that the school should be called St John the Baptist School, and not Sampford Peverell School, thereby connecting it with the Anglican Church rather than the Parish. This can be seen in Ada Morgan's bookplate of 1884.

> August 8th 1884
>
> ## SCHOOL OF
> ## S. JOHN THE BAPTIST,
> ## SAMPFORD PEVERELL.
>
> Ada Morgan

Ada Morgan's bookplate, 1884

Once the new school had been built, the Revd Ireland provided a house for the use of the Master: probably the Old Rectory, which had been used as the previous National School and where Mr Job had resided. After Mr Job was asked to leave, subsequent schoolmasters were housed in rented properties around the village. When Mr Smith arrived in 1902, the Revd Ireland dedicated one of his houses, Cross Hill, for the purpose of the schoolmaster's house.

Revd George William Rossiter Ireland, circa 1890

At a Vestry meeting on 16th April 1874 'It was agreed that parishioners should be asked to pay a voluntary rate of tuppence farthing in the pound for the supply of furnishings for the newly completed school, such furniture to belong to the Parish'. A memorandum in the Vestry Minutes of 1907 records the Revd Ireland's forthright comment: 'I wish to state that the present school was built entirely by me at my sole cost (the parishioners never giving a farthing) at a cost of £750 and on ground – not Church ground – belonging to me as a private person. NB The parish promised to give me £200 toward building a new school but they never, as I have said above, did anything of the sort.' The following day he did soften his statement a little by saying 'the Parish did give something for the furnishing of the school through a collection made for the purpose.' Having provided a new school and housing for the Master, there seems to be no record of the Revd Ireland being actively involved with the school once it moved to the new building.

Mr Job remained as Master until June 1875 when he was rather peremptorily dismissed by the Revd Ireland and his cousin, Curate of Sampford Peverell the Revd Philip Rossiter. He received a letter giving him three months' notice to leave the situations of schoolmaster and organist and 'deliver up quiet and peaceable possession of the Dwelling House and Garden which you now hold of us'. He was told that he was not at fault but the Revd Ireland had decided to give less money to the school. Ironically, two weeks later Mr Job received his teaching certificate from the Education Department. He did return one afternoon twenty years later in 1895 to look around the school.

Mr Job was followed as Headmaster by Robert Jackson who suffered frequent bouts of illness. He was obsessed with the children's cleanliness and tidiness, punishing them for coming to school with unwashed faces and uncombed hair. His certificate must have been low grade because he was not qualified to be in charge of pupil teachers. He lasted only fourteen months, dying in June 1877 of cirrhosis of the liver. His memorial tablet, which is to be found in the Parish Church, records his time as Master of the National School and adds this epitaph: 'He was a man of considerable talent both as a Musician and as a Schoolmaster of great zeal and energy of character and of a most forgiving and amiable disposition'.

The next four Masters, Thomas Lerwill, Walter Jewell, Charles Freeman and William Long, lasted one or two years each until Isaac Bamforth came in 1886 and he stayed for fourteen years. He employed his daughters: Mary as a second year trainee pupil teacher, followed by Gertrude in 1890, when the newly qualified Mary left for Salisbury, and by Maude in 1891. In addition to the Master there was an infant teacher. Mrs [Mary] Farr was first mentioned as such in the Log Book in 1874 when aged about 53, although she had started working as a school assistant a few years earlier. Having lived all her life in Higher Town, she had been described in the 1861 census as 'a plain needle woman'. This was useful when she taught sewing in school, although several other ladies were drafted in at various times when it was felt that the sewing had been below standard. Her career was interrupted on occasions by periods of absence. In 1877 she went to work at the East Devon School where she stayed for four months. On her return in January 1878 she spent several weeks working at the Rectory, whilst the pupil teacher took the two lowest classes. When she came back she not only taught the infants' class but cleaned the school. She continued to work on and off at the Rectory for several years, although the nature of the work is not recorded. On one occasion Mr Walter Jewell, Master from 29th April 1878, commented that 'the infants during her absence having lost in knowledge and many parents neglected to send their children for that reason'. Miss Radford was appointed as infant teacher in 1883 when Mrs Farr was 62.[16]

Pupil teachers were an important part of school life. The system was introduced in 1846. Bright pupils were chosen at the age of 13 and they taught and tested other children under the supervision of the teacher. If satisfactory, they sat the Queen's Scholarship to enter Teacher Training College. If they did not reach this standard they could teach as 'uncertificated' or 'assistant teachers'. Jane Membery was the longest serving pupil teacher. She started in February 1875 and left in 1880 to go to Fishponds Training College in Bristol, having gained a 1st Class Queen's Scholarship. Some pupil teachers started their careers as Monitors. Monitors were pupils who helped the Master and stood in for him during his absence when the pupil teacher was otherwise occupied. Samuel Dunn was appointed a monitor in 1878. Three years later the Managers (the Revd Ireland and the Revd Rossiter), satisfied with his moral character and the good influence of his parents, agreed to promote him to pupil teacher[17]. In 1892 Laura Salter started as a monitress in the infants' class receiving £2 a year. It was intended that this should be raised to £4 in 1893. At the same time the head pupil teacher was earning £18 a year, equivalent today to about £11,600.

Perhaps the most important person connected with the school in the last quarter of the 19th century was the Revd Philip Rossiter. After the opening of the new school building the Revd G W R Ireland seems to have relinquished day-to-day involvement. While still remaining a manager, he left the supervision of the school to his cousin Philip who visited the school regularly: two or three times a week, and sometimes more often. During his visits he would teach the Liturgy or read a religious text, mark and check registers and take an occasional secular lesson, especially reading. He often visited the parents of children who were absent and generally took an interest in their care and welfare. In May 1888 the Revd Rossiter married Miss Rendall, and the children were given a day's holiday[18].

School life was much more austere during the late 19th century than it is today. As the local children spent all their school years in the village school, sometimes more than 130 children were crammed into one room and more than thirty in the infants' class. Henry Buckingham, the Master in 1900, recorded 124 as being a poor average for a week and 144 as the highest. There were two fireplaces in the room, one at each end, but they were lit only when it was very cold. In 1877 the first

---

[16] Mary Farr is shown on the 1901 census as 'retired schoolteacher' living in Higher Town. She died in 1905.

[17] Samuel Dunn was the son of William Dunn, a shoemaker in Lower Town. His experience as a pupil teacher led to him becoming a schoolmaster in Eastbourne, East Sussex, (1891 census) and, later, a School Attendance Officer there (1901 and 1911 censuses).

[18] Philip Rossiter married Mary Eleanor Rendall, who we know was the daughter of an Army Officer (John King Rendall), and was the niece of the Revd George William Rossiter Ireland.

time they were lit was 20th November and in the following year the temperature dropped to 45 degrees Fahrenheit (7 Celsius) on 30th October before the fires were allowed. The HMI report in 1875 expressed the view that 'the new school room appears to be insufficiently warmed', and poor Jane Goffin had been unable to write because she had chilblains on her hands. Many children suffered with chilblains,[19] causing absences from school. Mr Bamforth commented that there were more children with 'chilled feet' in Sampford than there had been in Yorkshire where he came from.

Cleanliness around the school was very haphazard. In 1878 Mr Jewell appointed some children as 'sweepers' and they were allowed to attend school free of charge. When Mr Barrons, the school Attendance Officer, called at the school in the summer of 1896, he said that 'the offices [toilets] should be attended to every week this hot weather.' It is no wonder that the children were constantly absent with sicknesses of various kinds.

Arriving late at school was not tolerated. Mr Buckingham complained in 1900 that he had to send several children home because they had arrived after he had closed the registers. This occurred on a number of occasions both in the morning and afternoon, and one parent complained when her son was sent home for being late. He relented slightly eighteen months later when he reported that, although three girls had arrived just after he had closed the register, because they lived more than a mile from school, he let them stay with a warning that they would be sent home next time.

It is difficult to tell how long the school day was. It was divided into two halves with registers in the morning marked at 9 am. The morning and afternoon attendances varied quite considerably on some days, implying that several, if not all, of the children must have gone home for lunch. The school had no playing area, so if some of the children stayed they had nowhere to go apart from the schoolroom. There were no references to the time school finished in the afternoon, except on one occasion when extra time was given to spelling and the children were not dismissed until 4.40 pm. In October 1885 drawing lessons had been extended to 4.20 pm on a regular basis. As there was no electricity and they had only oil lamps, it must have been very difficult for the children to see their work in the winter.

Although when the school first opened the children must have used slates for arithmetic and writing, were they also using paper by the 1880s? The log book tells us some was delivered by Mrs Morgan, a village shop keeper in Higher Town, but was it used by pupils, teachers or for some other purpose? It was not until 1900 that the Inspector recommended the use of paper books instead of slates for Standard I.

---

[19] An itchy, purple red swelling, usually on a toe or a finger, caused by a reaction to cold temperatures especially in children and elderly people.

There were six Standards of Education, the details of which were contained in the Revised Code of Regulations 1872 which supplemented the 1870 Act. They referred to the attainments that children were expected to achieve in arithmetic, reading and writing as they progressed from Standard I onwards[20]. Religious Instruction was an important part of the school day, for which there was an Annual Diocesan Inspection. Singing and sewing were also on the school curriculum, as were history and geography. The first reference in the log book of an annual inspection is in

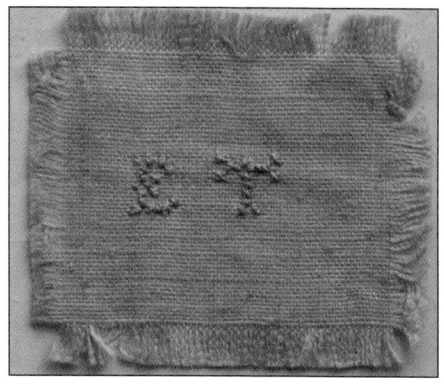

Sample of Standard 1 needlework from a Victorian Devon schoolgirl

1878. The report stated that 'This school is very low in attainments and numbers. I trust that under a new Master the results may be more satisfactory.' Under the new Master, Walter Jewell, the following year's report was slightly more detailed, with a few subjects cited as 'fair' and saying that the school had 'improved considerably in attainments and order since last inspection.' As the century progressed so the HMI inspections became more comprehensive, with subjects and teachers both being assessed. As an example, in 1895 the report said 'the spelling and writing generally might be stronger, but the children have passed on the whole a creditable examination. History has been substituted for English with very fair success, but an effort should be made to link together the stories read, so as to give the children a more connected view of the subject. The children are well under control and are interested in their work.'

In 1882 the Mundella Code was introduced, which had three aims[21]. It tried to broaden education beyond reading, writing and arithmetic by recognising for the first time that infants needed 'manual employments and organised play as devised by Froebel'[22]. It gave greater scope and variety to the list of optional or specific subjects for use in the higher classes. Until then the government Grant had been based purely on exam results, but the Code introduced a Merit Grant rewarding other forms of excellence. In January 1883 the new Master, William Long, bought

---

[20] See Appendix 3 on Standards of Education at the time.

[21] Anthony Mundella was a Liberal Member of Parliament and an early advocate of compulsory education in England.

[22] Friedrich Froebel 1782 – 1852 was a German educator who believed children should be able to grow up naturally without superfluous adult constraints. He valued highly play encouraged by a stimulating environment, believing that, through such free activity, the child would develop his thoughts and feelings in a spontaneous and genuine manner.

two new sets of reading books, a set of Geographical readers and Cassell's Historical Readers for Standards 4, 5 and 6 'as required by the new Code of 1882.' These were followed by 'sheet music on Hullah's System'[23], and 'Moffat's Box of Form and Colour for Infants'. Eventually in 1884 it was found 'necessary to slightly alter the timetable in order to fulfil the requirements of the new Code'. In December 1884 the Merit Grant was reduced from 'Good' to 'Fair', because the HMI found weaknesses in the teaching of infants and in sewing generally. Unfortunately, Mr Long suffered in consequence, as a large portion of the Grant was his salary.

Several Acts were introduced around this time, which were mainly concerned with the leaving age of the children. In the Elementary Education Act of 1880 local authorities were obliged to make bylaws requiring compulsory school attendance between the ages of 5 and 10. Poorer families found this very difficult as they needed their children to work for extra income, and although Attendance Officers often visited homes of absentee children, it usually proved ineffective. One parent, Joseph Salter, was summoned for neglecting to send to school his son Joseph, aged 9, who had attended only twelve times out of a possible forty eight. Mr J Frost, School Attendance Officer, proved the case and the defendant, who did not appear, was fined 2/6d. Children under 13 who were employed had to have a certificate to show they had reached the 'Educational Standard'. The 1891 Elementary Education Act stated that elementary education would be provided free. Ten shillings a year would be paid by Parliament for each child aged over 3 and under 15 attending an elementary school. The weekly fees for infants had been raised to 2d in September 1890, so this fee lasted for only one year. When the school reopened after the harvest holiday on August 31st 1891 there was poor attendance. Mr Bamforth thought this was due to free education starting the following day, although notice had been given that no fees would be charged that day. In 1893 the minimum leaving age was raised to 11 and extended to include blind and deaf children, who had previously had no official education. The school leaving age was raised again (to 12) in 1899.

In 1888 poor Lily Holloway's mother 'wishes Lily not to be pushed with her work and hopes she may not pass her examination, for, should she, the Guardians will stop her pay and she is only 9 years old.' (The widowed Mrs Holloway was receiving financial support from the Guardians of the Poor in respect of her children, but only whilst they remained at school.) Her request must have been successful because two years later Mr Frost gave 1/8d each in school fees for Lily and Hetty Holloway and William Sully. Unfortunately this was the last time for the two girls as Lily was now over age and Hetty, as the youngest child, received no fee. Sadly

---

[23] John Pyke Hullah (1812-84) was one of the leading figures in the 'sight singing mania' which became prominent in the 1840s. For more information, see the records of the City of London School at their web site http://www.jcc.org.uk/25th Anniversary/From-the-Archives/The start of music at CLS.aspx. accessed June 2012.

William Sully left school two years later to go to the workhouse in Tiverton. During the last decade of the nineteenth century, as the school leaving age was raised, it must have been increasingly difficult for parents to afford to keep their children at school. In 1899 the entire Parker family left for the workhouse because their father had run away from home. Older children were leaving school either to find work or to help parents at home. In Mr Bamforth's words 'some of them not seeming to care for their education now that they are 13 or 14 years old'. A parent, Mr White, stated that he will have 'to keep Harry home after this week as their servant is leaving'. Two Standard V children, who were possibly only ten years old, also left school in 1891, William Elworthy to learn his father's trade as blacksmith and Emma Collard to help her mother. On the other hand Harriet Parkhouse and Mary Hellier were withdrawn from school by their parents because their sewing was not up to the standard for their age.

Lady Day, on the 25th March, was traditionally the day on which agricultural labourers were hired for the year. Many remained with their previous employer but for those who did change, it would also mean moving home. It is first mentioned in the log book in 1886 because a number of children, whose fathers were dairymen, left the school at that time.

There were occasions when the children had some light relief from the formality of school routine. They gave several concerts to raise funds for the school library and other expenses. The school was closed for the afternoon on at least one occasion in 1887 when a platform was prepared for the 'Joy Symphony'. A school treat was celebrated at the beginning of the Harvest Holiday in July, when prizes were distributed. The school treat in 1889 was recorded in detail:

> 'The children assembled at the School at 1-45. Marched to Church at 2-30 – singing Onward Xt'ian Soldiers – several carrying banners. Children's Choral Service at 2-30 – preacher Revd Cappel Cure *[believed to be the Revd Edward Capel Cure, Vicar of Bradninch, Devon]*. After service – tea on the Rectory lawn – then prizes distributed – after which there were sports etc. in Mr Bowden's field, - the children thoroughly enjoying themselves, - being dispersed soon after 8, - after singing the National Anthem and the Evening Hymn.'

After the Christmas holidays the Revd Rossiter gave new coins to those children who had attended for complete weeks during the previous year. £3 in new money was distributed in 1885 to encourage regular attendance, although many children continued to be absent during the first three months of the year. In 1888 Revd Rossiter also gave two boys 2/- each for keeping the books in their proper places but 'This 2 shillings would be reduced to 1/- in future'. After an arithmetic exam in 1874 oranges were given to the children who had completed their sums correctly and nuts were given to all the children. At Christmas 1901 each child was given a bun (from school funds) and an orange (from the Master), also paper toys from 'Sunlight and Mallins', a company of which we know nothing more.

The National School 1874 - 1902

The school closed for the day on 14th September 1892 for an annual outing to Teignmouth involving the choir and teachers. A number of children went to watch soldiers passing through the village on several occasions, and many children with their parents visited the Volunteers Camp at Willand in 1890[24]. A 'children's entertainment' took place a few days before Christmas most years. Whether this was by the children or for the children and parents is unclear, but it was 'thoroughly appreciated' and an address was given by an eminent person: in 1894 this was the Archdeacon of Exeter. An occasional Magic Lantern Show was given by the Revd Rossiter, and in July 1899 'an entertainment was given to the school children - lecture on the Phonograph, Ventriloquism by Mr Palma.'

School holidays were sporadic during the last quarter of the 19th century. To begin with, only one week was allowed for the Harvest Holiday in August, but it quickly became apparent that many children remained absent afterwards as they were still working in the fields. This holiday was gradually extended until it was five weeks in 1881. Even then many children would still be working in the fields right through September, causing the Attendance Officer to visit the families, with little effect. 'The half-crown fines for non-attendance seemed to be of little value'. The Christmas holiday lasted about two weeks, sometimes not starting until Christmas Day, while Easter was between a week and ten days, with older children attending Church each morning during Holy Week before the start of the holiday. Then they would have a week's holiday for Whitsun. There were up to twenty-four Saints' Days celebrated throughout the year, when the children would go to Church at 11 a.m. and be given a half-day holiday in the afternoon. A day off was often given for the annual Sampford Peverell Fair Day in April, and when it was not given the children went to the Fair anyway! Occasionally the school would be closed for a day for cleaning, which must have been a mammoth task, as it appeared to happen only once a year. Apart from 1885, when the Managers gave consent for no apparent reason that the school could close for eight afternoons, occasionally a day's holiday would be given for special events. The school broke up a day early for the Harvest Holiday in 1880 for the children to visit the Rifle Volunteers Camp in Uffculme. Later, in 1900, it closed for half a day for the celebrations upon the Relief of Mafeking[25]. Two royal events led to the children having a day's holiday. In 1893 Prince George, Duke of York, married Princess Mary of Teck, and many children with their families celebrated by going to sports held in Uplowman. A whole week's holiday was given for Queen Victoria's Diamond Jubilee in 1897.

---

[24] The Volunteer Force was a citizen army of part-time rifle, artillery and engineer corps, created as a popular movement in 1859 following fears of a French invasion. Originally autonomous, the volunteer units became increasingly integrated with the British Army after 1881, before forming part of the Territorial Force in 1908. Most of the regiments of the present Territorial Army Infantry, Artillery, Engineers and Signals units are directly descended from Volunteer Force units.

[25] During the Boer War in South Africa Mafeking was one of the British garrisons besieged by the Boers. There was national rejoicing when it was freed in 1900.

Nothing was recorded about how the event was celebrated, but it would be nice to think that the children might at least have had a tea party.

Annual day trips to the seaside began when Mr Bamforth became Headmaster in 1886 and there were two undertaken in that year. The first was on 16th July when the Church Choir was taken by the Revd Rossiter to Torquay, and the second was five days later when the Chapel Sunday School went to Exmouth. After that there seems to have been one outing each year, but only for the Church Choir. This was usually to Teignmouth, but sometimes they went to Dawlish and, on at least one occasion, to Weston-super-Mare. The children were presumably taken by train, which in itself must have been a treat. Unfortunately not all the children were included as they were all organised by either the Church or the Chapel until the Band of Hope took over in 1898. Perhaps the annual trips were an incentive for the children to go to Church or Sunday School. The Log Book for the 21st July 1898 records 'The Band of Hope children gone to Dawlish, considerably thinning the school'. These outings continued each summer until 1933, sometimes coinciding with the Sunday School outings. The Band of Hope, formed in 1847, was the first temperance society exclusively for children, with an active branch in Sampford Peverell. It was based on Christian principles, the members taking the pledge to abstain totally from alcohol.

The farming calendar played a very important part in families' activities during the year and children would help in planting and harvesting. As a result school attendance figures would fall drastically. In February and March turnips and potatoes would be planted; then the children would go back to school until June and July when the senior boys would be absent again, helping with haymaking. The picking of blackberries, apples, nuts and potatoes occupied September and October and in 1890 'all the Moor boys[26] spent the afternoon selling their garden produce.' Gathering acorns for pigs added to the absenteeism in 1896, while 1900 showed the first reference to the children picking water lilies for sale[27]. This would have entailed them leaning out of boats and using sharp knives to cut the tough stalks, which must have been hazardous work.

Many children lived a fair distance from school. Roads in those days were probably not much more than tracks, so any heavy frost, snow or rain would make them very difficult to negotiate, especially for children on foot. In 1887 the Revd Rossiter suggested that the school be closed because severe frosts had made the roads

---

[26] The 1891 Census for Sampford Peverell lists 6 properties named 'Moor Cottage' or 'Moor House' in what appears to be the Leonard Moor locality. Living in these houses in 1891 were a total of 9 boys of school age who may well be those referred to collectively as 'The Moor Boys'.

[27] Initially the Tiverton canal was used to ferry goods and stone for limekilns. However, once the commercial traffic of stone had finished on the canal, the 11 miles was leased to a gentleman by the name of Joseph Barrie for the commercial growing of lilies, which were sent to the Midlands or Covent Garden market, chiefly to make wreaths.

very slippery and almost impassable. Even when it reopened attendance was poor because many children were ill with 'bad feet'. For several years in the 1880s and 1890s the school had to close when heavy snow caused deep snow drifts. In 1891, a notoriously bad year, a very heavy fall of snow, drifting up to 7 feet deep in places, closed the school for a week in March. It was recorded that a huge blizzard hit the south of England on 9th March and lasted four days. Winds were so violent that more than a million trees were blown down and roofs were ripped off houses.

Needless to say, the log books record that the children suffered from many ailments, sickness and diseases, sometimes in sufficient numbers to close the school. In 1875 Mr R Bryden, a surgeon, thought it 'very advisable and necessary that the Poor School[28] should be closed' because of an epidemic of scarlet fever in the village. It remained closed for four weeks but even when some of the children had returned, great care was needed with those 'who had had the fever - they seemed to suffer in the head'. Five child deaths were recorded during June, July and August. Four of these children were under school age, but one, James Candy, a five year old, would have been at school. The policy of closing the school for four weeks seems to have been effective in reducing the spread of the disease.

Epidemics of disease are mentioned frequently in the school log books. Apart from scarlet fever these included measles, mumps, whooping cough, influenza and scarlatina, from which in 1894 young Lily Hayward was 'thought unlikely to recover', but fortunately did so. A measles epidemic in 1881 closed the school for a month, but when it reopened the children were still suffering from severe colds - so it closed again for another week. In 1890, when a similar closure happened, the Easter holidays were cancelled so that the school could make up for lost time. Both measles and mumps affected so many children in November 1896 that Dr Haydon, Medical Officer of Health to the Tiverton Rural Sanitary District Council,

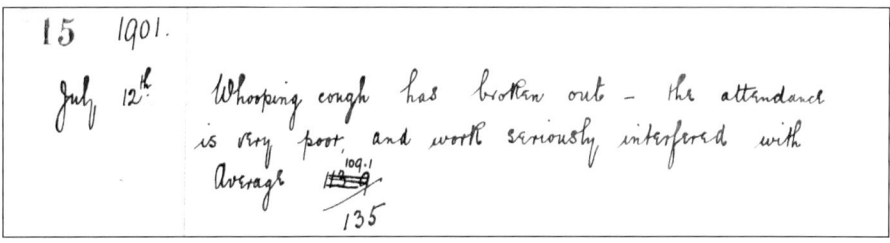

School Log Book entry for 12 July 1901

closed the school for four weeks, but had to extend it for an extra three weeks after Christmas. As recorded, at the start of every year many ailments and sicknesses affected the children, mostly unspecified except for colds and chilblains, or 'bad feet'. In 1898 a number of children were absent 'with bad places on their heads

---

[28] This was the alternative name for the National School at that time.

and faces', while Mr Bamforth (the Headmaster, 1886 – 1900) was 'still much troubled with rheumatism'.

Mr Freeman (master 1880 – 1882) rather optimistically opened a post office savings bank (known as "the Penny Bank") in the school in 1880. Initially there were no depositors and even a month later there were only two. Mr Freeman felt that the Penny Bank was not appreciated and, as it was not mentioned again, it must have been closed soon after. Mr Bamforth, who took charge of the school in 1886, started the Penny Bank again in 1891. This time there were seventeen depositors. Maybe this number reflected the fact that free education had started a month before. How it functioned was not explained, but periodically the Revd Rossiter used to 'take the money away'. Although money was scarce, the children were asked for donations to the Indian Famine Fund in 1897, and 7/10½d was collected on the first morning[29]. In 1899 the Revd Rossiter asked the children to collect for the Soldiers, Widows and Orphans. (This was at the start of the second Boer War in South Africa, which continued for three years). There is no record of the results of this appeal.

The National Schools had improved the education of British children, but by the end of the century the limitations were becoming apparent. A new approach was needed.

Cross Hill circa 1970: the Headmaster's house from 1902 until 1949

---

[29] Around 5 million people died in the famine of 1899-1900. This was partly the result of weather, partly because Indians were growing cash crops to sell to Britain - rather than for food. British efforts to relieve the suffering failed because of economic beliefs. The British Viceroy, Lord Lytton, saw food prices increasing, but thought that Indian farmers could thus make a profit and was reluctant to give free food. Sadly, the farmers themselves were starving. A small number made a profit, but millions more suffered and died. www.nationalarchives.gov.uk

Chapter III

East Devon County School: 1863 – 1907

At the same time as the setting up of the National School in Sampford Peverell, as described in Chapter II, there was interest in setting up private schools to educate the middle classes to equal the education provided by the independent schools. What is now West Buckland School in North Devon was founded as the Devon County School in 1858 by the Revd Joseph Lloyd Brereton, Prebendary of Exeter Cathedral and Rector of West Buckland, to provide a public school education (in the English sense of a private, fee-paying school) for sons of farmers and the middle classes. Its foundation stone was laid by Hugh, 2nd Earl Fortescue in 1860, who was a considerable philanthropist, and helped in setting up the school[30]. However, he died the following year, leaving his son Hugh, Viscount Ebrington, to succeed him as the third Earl Fortescue.

Two local rectors interested in education, the Revd Bere from Uplowman and the Revd Ireland from Sampford Peverell, started negotiations with Mr John Richard Chave who, realising that his debts were insurmountable, wanted to sell his Commercial and Mathematical Academy, based in Sheppard's Tenement (see

East Devon County School building in Lower Town, circa 1905

---

[30] The family seat of the Fortescues was, and is to this day, at Castle Hill, Filleigh, North Devon.

Chapter II). They appear to have been interested in the idea but to have 'dragged their feet' in actually doing anything about it. When the sale of Sheppard's Tenement and its contents took place in 1858, they did not acquire it. Instead, a group of philanthropic men took over the lease of another large vacant property in Lower Town, formerly occupied by Mr Samuel Lawrence's School (see Chapter I) and gave it the name of 'Sampford Peverell Middle Class Proprietary School' for the first few years of its existence.

In 1861 the Headmaster of the Proprietary School was John Robinson, aged 25, who came from Flintshire with his wife, Charlotte. He had two boarding pupils: John Williams, who came from Dorchester, and James John Norman, who came from London, and a general servant, Jane Webber, who was aged 29 and widowed. By December 1861 the school had 41 pupils. Mr Robinson was still the Headmaster in 1862, as we have advertisements for the various quarterly terms stating 'Applications to the Headmaster, Mr J Robinson'. He seems to have been in total charge of running the school, as even the butchers and bakers had to apply to him if they wished to be suppliers to the Middle Class School.

> **SAMPFORD PEVERELL MIDDLE CLASS PROPRIETARY SCHOOL.**
>
> **A SCHOOL** has been set on foot at the above place for the purpose of providing the Sons of the Middle Classes with a sound and Christian education equal to their wants. The plan on which it is founded is similar to that adopted at West Buckland and Chardstock. The course of instruction is intended to embrace, besides the Elementary part, Mensuration, Land Surveying, Book-keeping, Grammar, Geography, History, Singing, Chemistry, and Physical Science; also Latin, French, Algebra, and Euclid, where required. The following will be the scale of charges:-
>
> | A. | B. |
> |---|---|
> | FOR BOYS NOT NOMINATED BY SHAREHOLDERS | FOR BOYS NOMINATED BY SHAREHOLDERS |
> | Under ten years of age 22 gs. | Under ten years of age 20 gs. |
> | Above " " " " 25 gs. | Above " " " " 23 gs. |
> | Day Pupils 6 gs. | Day Pupils 5 gs. |
>
> The only extras to be Washing, Medical attendance, Instrumental Music, and Drawing to be supplied on the terms of their respective Masters.
>
> The School has been established partly by Donations, but chiefly by Shares. Every two Shares entitle to one Nomination.
>
> Suitable premises have been secured, and the School will open towards the end of July.
>
> As the Shares are not yet filled up, any persons wishing to become Shareholders, as well as any parents who wish to send their sons to the School, are requested to apply as early as possible to the Secretary.
>
> Rev. C. S. BERE Uplowman, Tiverton.

Exeter Flying Post, 13 June 1860

The third Earl Fortescue, as patron of the school, continued his father's philanthropy and had considerable correspondence with the Revd Charles S Bere, Rector of Uplowman, and secretary of the Sampford Peverell school, who wanted to change the existing name, the Middle Class Proprietary School, to East Devon County School. Earl Fortescue writes, 'Of course, you have an incontestable right in law to call it the 'East Devon County School', without invoking the Royal Licence.' He lists

'County' as distinguished on the one hand from purely 'Commercial' and on the other hand from purely 'Diocesan' or Church of England education. He lists:

> '1) A County School's object is to supply a public want and is not a commercial speculation. 2) To this end it should comprise among its managers (the choice of the Head Master) men of high standing and large property in the County: not only as a guarantee for the reality and permanence with the prestige thereto attaching; but also for the appointment of the fittest, and not merely the most locally influential candidate. It should possess certain endowments for the benefit and encouragement of its scholars, in the shape however no way derogatory to their self-respect or that of their parents.'

Basically, the intentions of the County Schools were to provide for the sons of the middle class a school based on the same general principles, offering the same kind of education that the English public schools did for the higher classes. This education was to be 'on terms within the reach of the middle classes and which shall have special reference to the future occupations of the pupils.'

The setting up of a County School at West Buckland attracted a lot of attention and encouraged other efforts in the same direction besides those at Sampford Peverell. The question of applying for a Charter arose. This might apply only to County Schools in Devon but could possibly develop into a national issue. The suggestion was that each County School would have its own separate shares and liabilities, yet be connected with and subject to the same rules as a parent body, which would have to audit the accounts of its branches and receive their reports. Under the Charter, the Trustees might appoint (and dismiss) the Headmaster and decide the general education for each establishment through a permanent body of trustees established for

---

EAST DEVON COUNTY SCHOOL, SAMPFORD PEVERELL.

At a **SPECIAL MEETING,** held at the SCHOOL, SAMPFORD PEVERELL, DECEMBER 18TH, it was resolved that the Company, lately entitled the **MIDDLE CLASS PROPRIETARY SCHOOL COMPANY,** should be registered under the Company's Act, 1862, as the "East Devon County School Association limited". This Step has been taken in order to put the school on a parallel footing with the Devon County School, at West Buckland, and to extend its usefulness more widely over the East of Devon. The shares are £5. Mr. S. Watson, late of Battersea Training College, and Member of the University of London, has been appointed Head Master, in the room of Mr. Robinson. Two Scholarships of £5 per annum, one tenable for two years, the other tenable for one year, have been founded for the benefit of the School. The School will RE-OPEN JANUARY 16. For particulars, apply to the Rev. C.S.BERE, Uplowman, Or after JANUARY 12, to the Head Master.

Taunton Courier, 31 December 1862

the whole County, to be known as The County Association of Schools, in which the several district or branch schools should be represented. This Association might receive endowments for the benefit of all its branches collectively, independent of those which each possessed separately. Earl Fortescue was hopeful that Sampford Peverell and West Buckland would be able to be joined under such a Charter. At the time that the school at Sampford was known as the Sampford Peverell Middle Class Proprietary School, it was not registered or limited. The school had been hanging on in the hope of a union on a commercial basis with West Buckland, but when this proved impracticable, the shareholders wanted to fix on a name and register it as the East Devon County School, to give the school greater status than the local 'proprietary' title. There was much persuasive correspondence from the Revd Bere to Earl Fortescue before the peer was persuaded to permit the title. On December 18th 1862 a special meeting at Sampford Peverell was held, and it was resolved that the Middle Class Proprietary School should be registered in its new name under the Company's Act 1862 and the Limited Liability Act, as the East Devon County School Association, Ltd. The school was registered under the Limited Liability Act in its new name. (The record of this registration is actually dated 1863 in the National Archives at Kew.) It was felt that this would achieve several things; it would put the school on a parallel footing with the Devon County School (today West Buckland School) and it would open it up to a greater area of East Devon, which would put it on a much more secure financial footing.

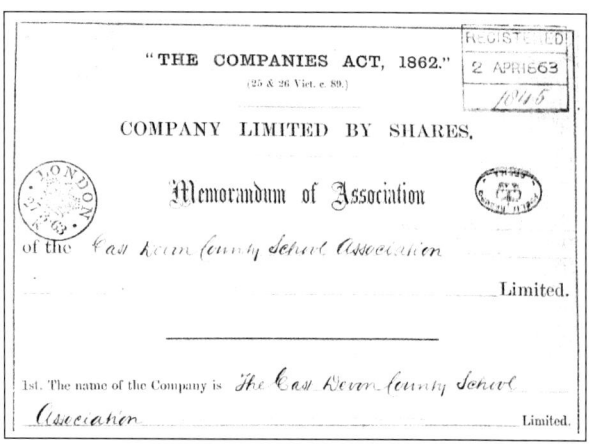

Company registration for The East Devon County School Association Limited

Limited Liability companies were still a new thing in 1862, having been introduced by the Limited Liability Act of 1855, and were regarded with some suspicion by potential investors. The shareholders of the original East Devon County School were the farmers and tradesmen of the neighbourhood, the parents of the boys. However, Revd Bere managed to issue shares to the value of £210 in the first few months, mostly to wealthy friends and relations, such as the Acland and Troyte families who had considerable local influence. Thus he was able to provide some working capital. By 1866, the share capital had risen to £900. The trustees were Sir Thomas Acland, the Third Earl Fortescue, Sir John Kennaway, E S Drewe Esq. and the Revd Bere, who was both school secretary and the equivalent of a bursar. On the occasion of the annual dinner, presided at by Sir Thomas Acland (as reported in the Western Times of 2 October 1866), the Revd Bere was commended by those present for his efforts in forming the school and for ensuring its continued prosperity. However, the school needed encouragement from men of high standing in the county. The Revd Bere appealed to Earl Fortescue to put some finance into the Sampford School and he did buy two shares at £10 each and Sir Thomas Acland[31] made a liberal contribution as well. Other benefactors were Sir J T Coleridge (1790 – 1876, judge and writer, nephew of Samuel Taylor Coleridge, 1772 – 1834); the Hon W W Addington (Viscount Sidmouth, MP for Devizes 1863) and Lord Palmerston (1784 – 1865, Prime Minister in the mid nineteenth century). By 1883 the share capital had risen to £2470 with just about every Earl, Baron and MP in Devon holding shares.

The Revd Bere was very keen for the Sampford Peverell school to have the title 'County' because he saw the school as 'a child of West Buckland' and said that he would 'be delighted if the child grows up like its parent'. It also claimed to be like West Buckland, where a permanent chaplaincy had been financed by Earl Fortescue, because it had, in effect, a chaplain for the school, as Revd Bere, having obtained permission from the Bishop (Henry Philpots 1778 – 1869) and the serving Rector of Sampford Peverell, preached to his boys in St John the Baptist Church in the village.

Besides the change of name there was a change of masters. The reason for this seems to have been because the number of pupils had 'fallen off in the past year in consequence of some dissatisfaction at the management of the late master,' referring to Mr Robinson. What the dissatisfaction with the management was is hard to imagine, as Mr Robinson went on to be the master of the Yorkshire School, Westminster Bridge Road, London, with Charlotte, his wife, as the matron. This school had about fifty boarders, nearly all from Yorkshire, so it was considerably bigger than the East Devon School and can only be regarded as a definite step up in his career.

At the end of 1862 the directors engaged as the new Headmaster Mr Samuel William Watson, who had won an excellent position at Battersea Training College and London University. The school reopened on 16th January 1863, and by the anniversary dinner in June that year the directors were able to report a marked improvement under Mr Watson's leadership. He was supported by Mr E Ramsay, who was thoroughly efficient, and both masters had gained 'the confidence of the shareholders and the affection of the scholars.'

---

[31] Sir Thomas Dyke Acland, 10th Baronet, born in 1787, was educated at Christ Church College, Oxford, graduating in 1808, gaining a Master's degree in 1814 and a doctorate of civil law in 1831.

At this dinner the Revd Canon Girdlestone from Halberton was the main speaker, and the Tiverton Gazette of 23 June 1863 recorded his speech as follows:

'Revd Canon Girdlestone on rising, said the very pleasing task had devolved upon him to return thanks for the honour they had just paid the Bishop and clergy of the diocese, and especially those who were present. They had done him the honour of coupling his name specially with this toast and with the work of education, and he accepted what they had done as a kind of challenge to say a few words on the subject of education generally, and specially of that portion of the educational subject which has brought them together beneath that roof today. They would not have any doubt upon their minds that the subject of education was one that was attracting a very large share of the attention of this country, from the legislature down to the lowest classes of the land. And there could be no doubt on any of their minds that education was a work which within the last 20 or 25 years had advanced with a rapidity that one could scarcely have anticipated.

Revd Canon Edward Girdlestone, circa 1850s
Courtesy of Deane Church, Lancashire

Beginning with the higher classes, the aristocracy and the gentry, it was impossible to shut their eyes to the fact that during the last 20 or 25 years – whether they took the universities or public schools, which were the feeders to them – the course of instruction given, as compared with that given when he was a young man, was almost as different as gold was from copper. He need not speak of the schools for the labouring classes. They knew the interest that was being felt the length and breadth of the land with respect to the education of the labouring classes. For his own part he held some sentiments that were perhaps opposed to those who sat at that table; he thought, and he had no fear of averring it, that the labouring classes of this country had been over-much educated. He did not see how it was possible for the son of a labouring man, who only earned 8s., 9s., or 10s. per week to be better fitted for the position of life which by God's providence had fallen upon him by being educated in those very high branches of instruction which for a very long time had been suggested in their national schools. He thoroughly rejoiced at the change which had come over the spirit of the Government in that respect, and that the feeling now was that the great thing to teach the children of the labouring poor was to read more – he meant with facility and with pleasure – in such a way that reading in after-life would not become a task, but in such a way as can be done with facility and pleasure; to write a good plain hand; to make use of the first few plain rules of arithmetic, and especially for the females, that they should be taught good plain needle-work – (cheers) – that all that fancy crochet work should be abandoned, and that they should be taught to cut out and make their husbands' shirts. (Loud applause). He was glad that rule had been adopted by the Government, and he hoped it would be in their national schools throughout the length and breadth of the land. (Hear, hear). He could only say that he had ruled that in the school of Halberton there should be no other instruction given. (Hear).

But if every other part of the community were to be educated, it stood plain that they, the farmers – the bone and sinew of the country – for he (Canon Girdlestone) reckoned the land, and those that cultivated it, as being the backbone of the country – it stood to their face that they must not be left behind in the race of education, and therefore it was that he now congratulated them upon their present meeting and the object for which they had met, and he would more heartily congratulate them upon the fact, which had come to his knowledge since he entered that room, viz., that this Middle Class School, whose object it was to educate the sons of farmers, had been originated not by the gentry of the land (although he was sure they took great interest in the work), nor by the clergy, although they were equally anxious to see it prosper, but that it had its origin in that which must always tend to its prosperity, in themselves. (Cheers). He was glad to be informed that it was originated by the farmers of the neighbourhood. (Hear, hear).

Still, those gentlemen, having as he might say, begotten the school, having wrapped it in its swaddling clothes, and having placed it in its cradle, could not even then bring up the child without some difficulties. The little bantling would be sure to have the complaints that were incidental to it. They would probably have great drawbacks, and some difficulties, but he relies upon the perseverance and sagacity of the farmers to carry on this school to its fullest prosperity. If they made 'a long pull, a strong pull, and a pull altogether' if they sent their boys to the school it must flourish. (Hear) But mark, they must not only send their sons to this school, they must take care that the course of education which was pursued in the school was one calculated for the position which their sons were, by the providence of God, destined to occupy. He had already said he thought the labouring classes had been too much educated; now don't let that be the fault of this school. Let the education in this school be good from its foundation: don't let them have mere shams and mere crams, but a sound education, which should fit the young farmer for becoming a better, sounder, and more prosperous farmer than his father or grandfather were before him. (Applause).

One thing there could be no doubt of – this applied to every sort of education, and to all schools alike; it was this – the foundation must be good, and in order for it to be good, it must be Scriptural. (Hear) What was the result if they had not a good foundation? He did not care what the superstructure was – whether of mathematics, chemistry, geology, or any other 'ology – unless the superstructure was built on the Rock of Ages it would tumble to the ground. Having said this, let him end by saying that, whatsoever superstructure they raised in their school, let them be sure that they built upon that only Rock upon which the superstructure could hope, under God's blessing, to be endowed. He wished prosperity to this school, and in any way he could give help to it, financially or otherwise, he should be most happy to do it.'

This speech met with great applause and the Revd Bere declaimed the school motto: 'Ora et Labora' (Pray and Work), which seemed to accord with Canon Girdlestone's sentiments, and it was obvious that the majority of those present agreed with him. An interesting comment was that chemistry was especially important for the sons of farmers.

Canon Girdlestone was later considered as the pioneer of the agricultural labourers' movement, as in 1866, when the cattle plague was at its height, he felt obliged to do something about the lot of the North Devon farm labourer. He had lived in Lancashire where farm labourers had been well paid, housed and cared for. The condition of the Devon labourers was a total contrast. He had asked:

> 'How is it possible on such wretched wages (7 shillings a week) for a man to house, feed and to clothe, not only himself, but his wife and children, and to pay in addition the doctor and the midwife, when their services are required: to provide shoes, fuel, light, such incidental expenses as school-fees, and in fact, many other items, which cannot be enumerated, but which enter, nevertheless into the cost of living'.

The Canon also made reference to the Bible, seeing the cattle plague as a judgment on farmers for treating labourers in this way. He wrote a letter to 'The Times' and received offers of employment for Devon labourers from all over England and Ireland, establishing a 'system of peasant migration'.

After Canon Girdlestone's speech, the Revd Bere admitted to teething troubles. The school had had a bad name and it was not easy to get a good name again. (There had been a lot of criticism of the previous master). He said that they were 'engaged in a religious work' and were 'not merely training boys to be mere machines, but to be Christian men, making the law of God the law of their life.' Mr Watson, the new Headmaster, said that his duty was to give a real, not a sham, education and that he tried to make boys 'sensible, real, true, honest, noble Englishmen.' (Exeter and Plymouth Gazette June 1863)

The course of instruction at the school, recorded in advertisements of the time, included the following:

> 'The Scriptures; English, including reading; writing; writing from dictation, and spelling, grammar, and analysis, composition, geography, and history; mathematics, including arithmetic, algebra, Euclid, and the higher branches, (book-keeping and land surveying are also taught to those who desire them); French; vocal Music and drawing. The following subjects are also taught at extra charge: Classics (Latin and Greek), German, and instrumental music'.

Sports available were rackets, fives, cricket and football. At this time, too, they had a master who could play cricket, for it appears that the Revd Bere 'could beat them all off his own bat'. The terms for the boarders were: 'Boys above thirteen, twenty-five guineas per annum; boys below thirteen, twenty guineas, with a deduction of £4 for weekly boarders; day boys, if nominated *(i.e. if the fees are to be paid by a shareholder)*, five guineas; otherwise, six guineas.'

The Exeter Flying Post of 24 June 1863 gave the following report on the School's Midsummer Examination:

> 'The work of the boys was tested by examinations held at the end of each quarter, in which some of the gentry and clergy of the neighbourhood generally take part. Her Majesty's Inspector, the Rev. W. Howard, also gave an annual inspection. Two scholarships have just been founded; to be competed for by boys who have been at least six months in the school; one founded by Sir T. D. Acland, Bart., of £5 for two years, the other by the Rev. C.S. Bere, of £5 for one year. Prizes of books are also awarded to those who had distinguished themselves at the examinations. The result of the examination on Friday is as follows: First class 1st Prize, with Sir Thomas Dyke Acland's scholarship, Edward Wilmet (Land and the Book[32]); 2nd prize, with Revd C.S. Bere's scholarship, John Burrough (Longfellow's Poems); both books were very handsomely bound...'

In The Exeter Flying Post there was a notice in January 1865 that the value of the scholarships had been increased in value to £30, which would be competed for at Midsummer. In June 1864 there was an article in the Exeter Flying Post about the annual meeting for the distribution of prizes at the East Devon County School which reads:

> 'On this occasion considerable gloom was thrown over the proceedings in consequence of a distressing domestic bereavement which had befallen the chief promoter of the school, the Revd C. S. Bere, in the death of his sister, whose estimable character and charitable disposition had endeared her to all classes in the neighbourhood of Uplowman, who had expired early that morning after a very short illness.'

The meeting was not postponed because all the arrangements were in place and, particularly, an excellent dinner had been prepared! The chairman spoke of the 'painful event which had deprived the meeting of the presence of Rev C. S. Bere', and stated that the prosperity of the school could be attributed to him. Later, toasts were proposed to the Bishop and Clergy of the Diocese, stating that 'education must be connected with conscientious convictions of religion.'

Mr Watson moved on from the school after a relatively short time. By 1867 Robert Clouting was in charge, Mary his wife was matron, and their son Reginald was soon to become assistant master to cater for the ever increasing numbers in the

---

[32] Believed to be a book by William McClure Thomson, published in 1859 and entitled 'The Land and the Book: Biblical Illustrations Drawn from the Manners and Customs, the Scenes and Scenery, of the Holy Land'.

school. By 1873, the staffing had expanded to include the Headmaster and four other resident masters.

Throughout the history of the East Devon County School the Revd Bere had had the education of the pupils at the heart of everything, and at the beginning of 1868 he felt moved to write a long letter to the editor of 'The Western Times' defending the school against some criticism that the subjects taught were not suited for boys whose future life would be of a commercial nature. The claim was that a classical education was being taught, but Revd Bere refuted this. He maintained that rather than teach a small amount of Latin which would not benefit the boys in the future, French was taught instead. Were a boy to need the use of French later in life, he could build on the grounding he had had. Latin was, however, an optional extra but at the time of writing the letter there was no boy in the school who was learning the language. The other criticism was that the directors interfered too much. Revd Bere defended this by saying that they had absolute trust in Mr Clouting, the Headmaster, 'whose whole heart and soul is in his work'. He had the confidence of both the parents and boys, and the expected increase in pupils was the best guarantee that the directors had got 'the right man in the right place.' It would certainly appear that the Cloutings were popular with the pupils, because upon the occasion of Mrs Clouting's birthday in April 1879, they presented her with a gold brooch.

In 1871 the dividend paid on the shares was 3½ per cent, and in 1876 the directors advertised to have additional shares taken up in order to increase the accommodation for teaching in the school. An acre of ground adjoining the building had been purchased for this purpose. Originally the school had purchased the premises at a cost of £800. It had also added a large schoolroom costing £250. It comprised a substantial house and the schoolroom and had all that was absolutely necessary for an educational establishment. It had healthy rooms, a good cricket ground, a bathing place and a fives court. White's Directory 1878 says that 'the buildings are admirably adapted to their purpose and attached are a good rackets court, fives court etc.' and that the attendance for the last few years had been eighty boys.

> **TO BUTCHERS.**
> PERSONS desiring to supply the East Devon County School, Sampford Peverell, with MEAT during the next half-year are requested to send their Tenders to the SECRETARY on or before FRIDAY, the 16th instant.

Western Times, 6 July 1875

At an anniversary dinner in 1876 Earl Fortescue lamented the difficulty in finding teachers for middle-class schools who came from the same society as their pupils. The answer was to give the teachers better pay to encourage people of that class to choose 'the tiresome and monotonous work of a pedagogue'! A working class boy might well go into teaching in the elementary schools, as he would earn more than he would by following his father's trade, and his social status would be 'decidedly superior'. Earl Fortescue also spoke about the danger of allowing educational attainments and mental gifts to gain an undue preponderance over muscle in the officering of the army. This was followed up by Major Troyte referring to 'poor little beggars' of officers who had passed in education, but who would vanish after a fortnight's camping. The writer of the article, in the 'Plymouth and Exeter Gazette', then reminded his readers after this comment of 'A certain little beggar of an officer' called Sub-Lieutenant Napoleon Bonaparte formerly of the French Artillery'!

In January 1877 tragedy struck the Clouting family when Reginald, who by this time was second master at the school, died at the age of 24. The Church burial register records the cause of death as typhoid (a bacterial infection acquired from food or water contaminated with human sewerage). No mention of this is to be found in contemporary newspaper reports about his untimely death.

In December 1879 the prize-giving and dinner was a smaller occasion, on account of the general depression of trade, and only two directors were present. There were two small money prizes presented by Major Troyte for those who were successful on the rackets and fives courts. The Revd Bere exhorted the boys who were leaving to use their education well and not to imagine that it had finished on leaving school. By 1880 Mr Robert Clouting had moved on and Mr Thomas J B Sandercock had taken his place. Mr Clouting was praised by the directors, who now had every confidence that the new Headmaster would carry the school forward. Mr Sandercock came with experience of agricultural chemistry, a quality which recommended him highly to the directors. A subsequent advertisement for the school makes special emphasis of 'the teaching of Elements of Agricultural Chemistry'.

The school was closed for a time because of an epidemic, which had 'not been generated in, but imported into it' but it reopened in January 1882. After this it was deemed necessary to build a sanatorium, but for the present a cottage was rented for the purpose. The whole premises had to be disinfected, on the orders of the Medical Officer of Health, who reported that they were 'large, commodious, and well-drained.' In July of that year a bazaar was held on the cricket field of the school to raise funds for the sanatorium, which cost £300. Mrs Sandercock was the matron and housekeeper, who advertised for a 'good plain cook and two respectable housemaids'.

The school quite often put on entertainments in the lower schoolroom. There were two such on successive evenings in December 1882 when the boys put on 'Box and Cox' and 'The Blind Beggars'[33]. Mr Sandercock designed and built the stage, described in 'The Western Times' as 'a little gem', entirely on his own, and the boys were praised for keeping up for several minutes without speaking an amusing by-play, 'a hard feat for boys to accomplish'.

Mr Sandercock left the school in March 1883, to take up another Headmastership at Ascham School, Dawlish. He was succeded by Mr John Hamilton Edmonds. During his tenure, in January 1885 there was an announcement in The Western Times about Honiton Grammar School which read 'It is arranged that the school be removed for a term to the premises of East Devon County School.' No explanation is given in the announcement but there was an outbreak of smallpox in Honiton in the previous December.

Initially, as stated earlier, the directors of the company were 'men of property and standing' and they took a considerable interest in how the school was run. As time moved on, however, it would seem that their involvement was reduced, such that in 1879 only two of the directors were present at the annual prize-giving and dinner. The Revd Bere himself, who had been the backbone of the establishment and Secretary of the school, was gradually reducing his commitments, owing to his impending move from Uplowman Parish to Morebath Parish. By October 1884 he had relinquished his role as Company Secretary to Richard Chave Merson, a local surveyor. It would appear that many or all of the remaining 'old guard' directors decided to resign at about the same time. The Revd Bere moved to Morebath where he died three years later at the age of 60.

One of the new directors was Binford Sellwood, a farmer and tannery proprietor from Cullompton, who was appointed as the Chairman. The new directors must have reviewed the arrangements and decided that it was no longer necessary to run the school as a limited company, and set about re-privatising it. At a shareholders' meeting in August 1884 a Special Resolution was passed 'That the affairs of the company be wound up voluntarily and the Premises offered for sale.'

Later it transpired that the limited company was not, in fact, the owner of the school premises, which remained in the name of the Middle Class Proprietary School. Consequently the directors were unable to act upon the Special Resolution to sell the premises. A second meeting was convened in November 1884 and it was resolved that the shareholders would give up all claim to the school premises, provided that the trustees of the Middle Class Proprietary School (who may have

---

[33] Box and Cox is the title of a comic play (1847) by J M Morton, in which two characters, John Box and James Cox, unknowingly become tenants of the same room, each using the facilities at different times, unknown to the other until the dénouement. The Blind Beggars is an ancient tale in which one character deceives two (or three) blind beggars by offering money to them, telling each that one of the others has it. The beggars go to an inn, and feast on the supposed money, only to find that no-one has it and they have been duped. They get revenge upon the perpetrator in various ways, depending upon the particular version of the tale. That performed by the Sampford boys is unknown.

been the same as the original East Devon County School Association Limited's directors) would take on the liability for the mortgage of £2700. The winding up of the company now proceeded, with the secretary, Richard Chave Merson, appointed as Liquidator. We do not know how much money there was to return to the shareholders of East Devon County School Association Limited, but there was presumably some, perhaps even a surplus over and above what they had invested. The final meeting was held in May 1885, at which the liquidator's accounts would have been presented.

It seems probable that the school's trustees were then eager to release themselves from the liability of the mortgage at the earliest opportunity and set about finding a new Headmaster willing to take on the lease and mortgage. They managed to find Mr William Goring Benge. He came from the Middle Class School in Barnstaple and took over the role in the spring of 1886. The annual Land Tax Returns until 1886 record the Proprietary School's trustees as both owners and occupiers of the property but thereafter, until the school's eventual demise, Mr Goring Benge is mentioned as the sole proprietor. This, ironically, exposed the school to the same financial risks that had beset J R Chave over twenty years earlier, and from which Revd Bere had worked so hard to rescue it.

Mr Benge now had complete control over the future direction of the school. During this time the school had an average of eighty pupils, about twenty of them being boarders and coming from as far afield as India and Ireland. Mr Goring Benge's wife was the matron, and they had two daughters. In September 1886 the school was advertising for girls, claiming excellent accommodation for boarders, spacious premises, grounds of six acres, and a modern education, with masters for important subjects, which implies that women were considered to be inferior as teachers. A similar advertisement is for boys, claiming splendid accommodation for boarders with separate beds or private rooms. There was a playground of an acre, and four acres of field. The bathing area is now described as a 90 foot swimming bath, and agricultural chemistry and French are stressed as important subjects. Parents are invited to inspect the premises and there is a preparatory class for little boys. In the 1891 census the youngest boarder is only seven,

> **EAST DEVON COUNTY SCHOOL for GIRLS, Sampford Peverell, to be OPENED SEPTEMBER 13th.** The Principal will receive parents and show premises any day after September 6th.
>
> EAST DEVON COUNTY SCHOOL, SAMPFORD PEVERELL.
> Established 30 Years.
>
> **S**PLENDID ACCOMMODATION for Boarders, separate beds or private rooms, modern education, playground one acre, field four acres, swimming bath, agricultural chemistry, French daily. Department for young ladies. Preparatory class for little boys. Parents are invited to inspect premises. Pupils entered at any time. Fees, 8 guineas and 9 guineas per term.
> Prospectus of the HEAD MASTER.

Exeter Flying Post, 7 September 1886

but no girls are recorded as boarding. The advertisements at this time make capital of the care and attention given to the pupils, stating that meals are taken at the Headmaster's table and that the best food is supplied, with a milk diet daily, and claiming that the limestone spring water promotes bone growth and that the healthy district is good for weakly boys. Interestingly the fees did not increase over the following decade. Advertisements in 1900, for example, continued to show the level of fees to be eight to ten guineas a term, while at the same time boasting many successes in the chosen careers of some former pupils, such as the civil service, the stock exchange, banking and veterinary science.

> **EAST DEVON COUNTY SCHOOL,**
> **SAMPFORD PEVERELL, TIVERTON**
>
> Established 50 Years.   Six Scholars
>
> A Home School with Family Life. Only 25 Boarders received, individual attention guaranteed.
> Four persons entirely engaged in superintending these pupils. Best Food supplied. Meals taken at Head Master's table. Milk diet daily. Lime Rock Spring Water promises bone growth. Healthy district for weakly Boys.
>
> 100 Successes. Two Passed recently as Accountants. Salaries £40 and £50. Premises cost £6000. Playgrounds. Fields. Swimming Bath. 12 Miles Boating.
>   Fees **8** and **10** Guineas

Western Times, 2 November 1900

It seems that Mr Benge retired from teaching sometime towards the end of the summer term of 1905, although there is no evidence of a leaving celebration. From August of that year there are frequent advertisements stating the same thing, namely 'Goring Benge, the Head master of the above school for 20 years, now retires and wishes to receive four pupils in his private house.' How successful these advertisements were we do not know but at the same time it appears that Goring Benge was trying to sell the premises. In late 1905 and early 1906 there was discussion about the school by Devon Education Committee. A sub-committee had obviously looked at the premises with a view to its being suitable for 'children of weak mind'. In February 1906 Sir Redvers Buller[34] stated that the sub-committee thought so much alteration

> **EAST DEVON COUNTY SCHOOL, SAMPFORD PEVERELL.**
> GORING BENGE, the Head Master of the above School for 20 years, now retires, and WISHES TO RECEIVE FOUR PUPILS in his Private House.
>   Backward or Delicate Boys would be carefully studied. Grounds spacious. Own Dairy. Boating and Swimming.

Tiverton Gazette, 22 August 1905

---

[34] General Sir Redvers Henry Buller, (1839–1908), was born at the family seat of Downes, Crediton. He was awarded the Victoria Cross for bravery in the South African war of 1878, and a statue of him stands today in Exeter.

would be necessary that it would be more economical to build a new school than to buy this one.

Goring Benge from this time on placed many 'For sale' advertisements in the local press. He was selling various horses and ponies, together with their gigs and harnesses, and cows and calves. As early as August 1905 there was to be a big two day clearance sale by Helmores. All manner of things were to be sold: good quality furniture, oil and water-colour paintings, books, kitchen and dairy utensils, 'the appendages' of thirty rooms, as well as horses, ponies, heifers, pigs, poultry and machinery and implements. Goring Benge still had plenty of livestock in July 1906, as the advertisements were still regularly placed and there is a report of a cow being found lying dead in the yard by one of Goring Benge's employees. The police were called to this incident and the veterinary surgeon ascertained that the cow had died through eating laurel leaves that had been placed in the yard - whether with criminal intent or through ignorance is not recorded.

> **EAST DEVON COUNTY SCHOOL, SAMPFORD PEVERELL**
> 3 Miles from Tiverton Junction Railway Station, 5 Miles from Tiverton.
> Important SALE on WEDNESDAY and THURSDAY, September 13th and 14th, of well-made furniture in mahogany, oak, walnut, satin, and other woods; Oil and Water Colour Paintings, Etchings, and Books, Kitchen and Culinary Requisites, Dairy Utensils and Effects; the appendages of 30 rooms; also the Horses, Ponies, Heifers, Steers, Pigs, Poultry, Machinery, Implements, &c. FREDERICK JOHN HELMORE has been favoured with instructions from GORING BENGE, ESQ. (who intends to retain only a few private pupils) to submit by PUBLIC COMPETITION, on the dates above mentioned, commencing each day at 12 o'clock noon.

Exeter Flying Post, 29 August 1905

In August 1906 the wedding of Edith Hope Benge, the younger daughter of Goring Benge, took place in St John the Baptist Church, Sampford Peverell. The groom was Douglas Gerald Gilbert of Roborough School, Eastbourne. It was a very grand affair and, out of respect for Mr Benge's standing in the village, the local people attended the church in large numbers. In the evening Mr Benge held 'open house' for all to attend in the grounds of the school. The bride's wedding dress and bouquet are described in great detail in the local press, and the presents were said to be numerous and costly. It seems that Mr Benge liked opening his house to the village people, as on New Year's Day of 1907 he held a dance and provided all the refreshments for all to enjoy. He probably felt safe in doing so as it was reported that over the Christmas festivities there had not been a single case of over-indulgence in alcoholic beverages in Sampford Peverell!

Eventually the school was bought in August 1907 by the Church of England Waifs and Strays Society, with a view to converting it into an industrial school where boys of over 14 might be taught carpentry, gardening and other trades. Goring Benge was definitely a local worthy, for besides being the Headmaster he was also a councillor, voicing his opinions quite strongly at Council meetings and most notably delivering a long speech on free trade versus protection in 1904. He remained in Sampford Peverell for some time after the sale, stirring up trouble on the Parish Council and complaining about the fact that he had paid for a main sewer to be put in and others had connected into it without paying him anything. He was claiming £15 from the council but he announced that he was shortly to leave the neighbourhood, which may have been a relief to all concerned. The move took him to Tetbury in Gloucestershire, where he continued to play an active part in community life.

Chapter IV

The Church of England School: 1902 to 1944

By 1900 there was a crying need for reform and coordination of the national system of education. Voluntary elementary schools, funded by subscriptions from local benefactors or religious groups, preferred by the Conservative government of the time, were being out-performed by Board Schools whose funding came from the rating system.

The Education Act of 1902, known as the Balfour Act[35], abolished the Board Schools, the very popular education system set up by the 1870 Elementary Education Act. In their place, Local Education Authorities (LEAs), under the auspices of the County Councils, set the local tax rates, which funded the education system. They were in charge of appointing properly qualified teachers, controlling expenditure and supplying books and equipment. The LEAs would also carry out inspections of school buildings and would receive four shillings a year per pupil from central government to ensure that children aged 5 – 14 years received education. The Act also provided funds for denominational religious instruction in Voluntary Elementary Schools, owned mainly by the Church of England and the Catholic Church. Denominational schools continued to provide and maintain their own buildings, and each denomination was to be responsible for religious education.

The Act proved highly controversial, developing into a major political issue. Nonconformists, radicals and Liberals were opposed to the Act on the basis that ratepayers' money would now be spent on Church of England schools. Liberal politician John Clifford urged passive resistance by the withholding of rates[36]. Many law-abiding citizens preferred to go to prison rather than pay rates which would fund the teaching of a religion they believed to be wrong, or benefit schools over which they had no shadow of control. Nationwide, 170 people were imprisoned and many others had goods seized and auctioned. Locally, Chumleigh vicar, the Revd Veale had a set of coronation spoons sold for 18 shillings when the amount due on his rates was 12 shillings. Three years later in 1905 a Cruwys Morchard man, Mr William Lake, had his oats sold for 2/5d per bushel.[37]

---

[35] A J Balfour was Conservative Prime Minister from 1902 to 1905
[36] John Clifford was President of the National Council of Evangelical Churches and such a strong advocate of resistance that he withheld payments and had his goods restrained. http://encyclopedia.jrank.org/CHR_CLI/LIFFORD_JOHN_1836_.html;accessed November 2012.
[37] A bushel measure is equal to 8 gallons or about 36 litres.

Antagonism between Nonconformists and the Church of England continued nationwide and locally. In 1907 the establishment of a Sampford Peverell Charitable Trust was proposed, with a trust fund of £69 10s 1d from the sale of the school house (The Old Rectory) sold thirty years earlier. The trustees were to be the vicar, two churchwardens and one representative of Devon County Council (DCC), thus giving the Church Authorities the balance of power. The yearly income from the trust was to be awarded as prizes to the children of the parish for attendance at school and at a 'Sunday school in connection with the Church of England'; to assist the child with continuing education or with the cost of 'an outfit on entering upon a trade or profession or otherwise for his or her special benefit'. Methodist minister the Revd Cowdell spoke at a public meeting in the Methodist Sunday School room and summarised the unfairness of such a scheme, which made the award of prizes to children dependent on their religion rather than on studiousness and diligence.

In 1903 Sampford Peverell school, now the responsibility of the County Council, had its first body of Managers which included two representatives of DCC and two from the Church of England. The Managers were responsible for regular inspections and the appointment of assistant and pupil teachers. The appointment of these teachers was not always straightforward. In December 1904 there is a reference to Revd P Rossiter[38] going to see the Secretary to the Education Committee of DCC about filling two vacancies at the school, 'adverts having proved abortive'.

Regular inspections were carried out by both the County and the Diocese. County inspections commented that standards in Arithmetic were 'showing weakness' and in Repetition[39] 'some children were backward'. Diocesan inspections commented on things such as Discipline and 'Tone'. A particularly pleasing Diocesan report in September 1919 was as follows: 'The Headmaster and his staff deserve congratulations for the condition of the school. Combined with rare enthusiasm there is good intelligence. The older children have been taught "to think"'.

The School Year

In 1902 the school year commenced at the end of October, when children moved to the next Standard (see Appendix 3). The year was divided into five periods, with examinations being taken at the end of each one. Following the recommendation of the Education Committee, from 1913 the new school year began at the end of March. This did not necessarily coincide with the Easter holidays, which must have

---

[38] Revd Philip Rossiter was Rector of the Parish from 1908 - 1910, Chairman of the Managers and the owner of the school.

[39] Reciting hymns and texts.

been somewhat confusing. Then in 1935, another change brought the start of the new school year to September, with examinations taking place twice yearly.

At the end of the Christmas term book prizes were awarded for both secular subjects and Scripture. At the end of the year, the Managers awarded the school prize of a watch and chain to the boy or girl with the highest number of marks for conduct, examinations and attendance added together. Most children began school aged five as an Infant, and progressed through Standards I to VII, leaving at the age of fourteen.

Staff and subjects taught

At the end of March 1902 the Headmaster Henry Buckingham resigned at the age of 55, after just two years in post. Originally from Tavistock, the son of a school master, he conscientiously left detailed notes on the syllabus followed, the staff in charge of each class and even the songs being sung, which included 'The Hardy Norseman', 'Now From Every Bush and Tree' (a song sung in parts) and 'Rule Britannia!'

In addition to arithmetic, reading and writing, subjects on the timetable included: religious instruction and singing; moral instruction and training in citizenship (following a DCC syllabus); historical reading; natural phenomena; and, for the girls, the care of infants and domestic science - the latter taking place at the nearby village of Halberton. Handiwork subjects included bookbinding, raffia work and weaving, as well as needlework for the girls and woodwork for the boys.

Henry Buckingham's successor, who took up his post on 7 April 1902, was 29-year-old John Henry Smith. With his wife Mary and two children, Wilfred and Winifred, he moved into Cross Hill Cottage, the property designated as the Headmaster's house. The number on the roll at that time was 114.

Standards V, VI and VII, (the older pupils), were taught by Mr Smith himself, Standards III and IV by Miss Atkins while Miss Tapp, assisted by Agnes Saunders, monitress, took Standards I and II. Agnes later became a pupil teacher. Her training entailed receiving instruction from the Headmaster each weekday morning from 7 am to 8 am, assisting in the classroom for fifteen hours per week and spending eleven and a half hours a week on her own studies. Agnes must have been successful as a teacher, as she was still in post twelve years later, when the school choir sang at her marriage service in April 1914. On his first day Mr Smith recorded that the infants were under the charge of Miss Tucker, a pupil teacher, as 'a permanent member of staff hasn't yet been appointed'.

During the first few years of Mr Smith's Headship, there were several changes of staff, due to some temporary appointments and some staff moving away from the area. He also had to contend with the non-appearance of newly appointed staff, 'This being unfortunate, as the regular work of the school is being seriously interfered with'.

At the beginning of 1905, the school was forced to close for a week, 'as a replacement for a teacher had not been found; the Head being indisposed; and no experienced teacher able to be in charge of the school'.

From time to time members of the staff featured prominently in the Log Book. One such occasion, in 1905, followed a critical report by an Inspector, on the standard of darning holes in stocking web material: 'More attention must be paid to the direction of the selvedge in the various exercises'. In defence the Head remarked that the teacher had only recently changed the method of darning, 'the children having insufficient practice in perfecting the new style'. However, following some unexplained absences, and taking with her some of the school's materials, some of which were not returned, the same teacher resigned at the end of the year, the cost of the materials subsequently being deducted from her salary.

> 23. III. 04. H. M. Inspector last Wednesday were forwarded to Whitehall, and the following report was received today.
> "The darning does not satisfactorily fulfil the purpose of the exercise, viz, to teach the mending by darning of a fair sized hole in stocking web material.

School Log Book entry for 23 March 1904

In another instance the Log Book of February 1904 records a pupil teacher absenting herself for a week, but 'it would seem, however, that there was not sufficient reason for this continued absence, as from information received (partly from the corresponding manager) it would appear that she was sufficiently well on Monday to attend a dancing class - on Tuesday a confirmation class, and since then 'to sit with a girl friend recovering from an illness'.

Denis Cluett, a pupil in Mr Smith's time, remembered much about his years at the school, and wrote of it in his reminiscences (see the Society's publication "A Village Childhood"). He recorded that:

> 'After prayers in the morning the first period was always arithmetic when the Headmaster would set us some sums to do. While we were struggling with these, the Head would sit on a high stool at his desk and read the Daily Mail. At this time the Daily Mail always printed in it a humorous column on the leader page, and sometimes when the Head

found this article particularly amusing he would call for the attention of the class by striking a bell on his desk, and would read the article out aloud to us. Unfortunately, after reading the first two or three sentences he usually became quite incoherent with laughter, tears would roll down his cheeks and the more he read, the less we understood. Nevertheless we all felt duty bound to roll around with laughter, and some of the more exuberant spirits would deliberately fall off their forms in ecstasies of simulated mirth.'

Denis learned both arithmetic and reading by chanting. The teacher flicked the beads of an abacus along the wire, while the children chanted a counting rhyme. Alphabet chanting and cloth-covered reading books were the means of learning to read. By 1914, slates and chalk used for practising handwriting were replaced by copybooks and pencils. For Standards I to V, moral maxims and proverbs printed in copper plate script at the top of each page, were to be replicated on the page below. On Friday afternoons, the four classes joined together for singing. The standard song book, probably issued to all schools at that time, included songs such as 'Hearts of Oak', 'Men of Harlech' and 'God bless the Prince of Wales'.

After 29 years of Headship, Mr Smith resigned in December 1930, owing to continued ill health. Mr Percy James Voaden, who taught Standards III and IV and who had married another member of the staff, Florence Norman, temporarily took over the charge of the school until April 1931 when Mr Thomas John Samuel, affectionately known as Tom John, was appointed as the new Headmaster. Mr Voaden left his post in May 1931, to take up a new appointment as Headmaster in Newton St Cyres. Mrs Samuel soon became appointed as a permanent member of the staff. Mr and Mrs Samuel remained at the school until 1949.

The School Building

From its inception in 1874, all the children were taught in the one schoolroom, divided in two by a curtain. In 1905, the Education Board reported that the nature of the premises was 'a hindrance to good work but they understood that the main room would soon be divided by a partition, unless other plans were devised in the meantime'. Much discussion ensued as to who should pay for this, the school maintaining it should be responsible solely for the 'fixed portion', and the LEA paying for the partition itself. Similarly, letters were sent from the school in 1905 regarding the cost of re-casting the bell, which had recently been erected. 'Wear and tear', according to the Education Act of 1902, was deemed to be the responsibility of the LEA. We do not know who eventually paid! *[Nor is it recorded why the bell should need re-casting so soon after being erected.]*

Following in his cousin's philanthropic footsteps, Revd Philip Rossiter, the owner of the school, paid for a new room 20' x 22'[40], to be added to the school in 1909, just

---

[40] This was on the west side of the main building, now the school office.

Infants class, 1903 or 1904. Mr Smith on the left

Class 2, circa 1905. Mr Smith on the right

The Church of England School: 1902 - 1944

Class 3, 1909

Class 5, circa 1908. Mr Smith on the rightCourtesy of Tiverton Museum of Mid-Devon Life

a year before his death in October 1910. Despite a huge one third increase in area, no mention of the building appears in the Log Book except, 'there being a service of dedication on 1st September in the morning and the children were given a half day's holiday by the request of Revd Rossiter. The new furniture had not yet arrived, so the old desks were used; Standards III and IV using the room first'. The school could now accommodate 133 juniors and 32 infants.

A playground was also provided, with a solid wall separating the boys from the girls. Later, in 1914, 'the west yard, being bigger, was given to the boys; and the infant playtime started five minutes earlier to give them the playground to themselves'.

A former pupil, Jack Scorse, remembered that there were three classrooms when he started school in 1920. The infant room (the new classroom added in 1909) had three age groups - babies, 1st class and 2nd class - all being taught by Miss West. The middle room, now the library, accommodated pupils of Standards I and II who were taught by Miss Bailey. The main classroom, now the hall, was partitioned by a curtain hung on a length of piping. Standards III and IV were taught by Mr Voaden, on one side of the curtain, while Standards V, VI and VII, were taught by the Headmaster on the other side.

All Mod Cons!

In 1918 the then Chairman of the Managers, Revd J J Rees[41], replaced the original earth closets, that stood at the top part of the playground behind a brick wall, with buckets. He bought the buckets out of his own pocket and then applied for reimbursement from the LEA, but without success, despite some pleading letters to the Education Committee. The bucket closets remained until the 1930s when mains water came to Higher Town, which allowed the

> 18 October 1918
>
> Dear Sir,
> I shall be grateful if you can help me out of a difficulty. I have no funds whatever to keep this Church School in repair, but have hitherto paid all from my own pocket. I think it is most unreasonable for the Local Education Committee to refuse to pay for the sanitary buckets (kept entirely for use of the children) as stated in the enclosed letter. I also enclose a cutting from the Church Times which I think supports me. I sincerely trust you will see your way clear to give instructions to the Local Committee to pay the small sum in question.
> Thanking you in anticipation
> Believe me
> Very faithfully yours
> J J Rees.

Copy of letter from Revd Rees to LEA, 18 October 1918

---

[41] Revd John Jacob Rees was Rector from 1911 – 1940.

conversion to water closets. Wash-hand basins were also installed in the porch near the rear entrance to the school and Jack Scorse remembers filling buckets of water from a pump in Boobery [42] during his last year, in 1930. Mains drainage did not arrive until June 1942, when the Log Book quoted, 'Today the noise produced by road engine outside school necessitated modification of timetable and for work to be done outside away from the disturbance. The work was being done in regard to school sewer which was being connected up to the main drain'.

Electricity was installed in the school at the end of August 1931. Until then, to make best use of natural light, the afternoon timetable was altered during the winter 'to enable copybook lessons to be taken in the morning; the afternoon used for singing and oral lessons'. In 1936 facilities were further improved with the installation of a telephone, probably long before most pupils had one in their own home.

School Attendance

Prior to the 1902 Education Act the issue of attendance was left to the discretion of headmasters and teachers. Headmaster Henry Buckingham was particularly concerned with the low attendance at the school saying 'there is terrible indifference among some parents to the benefits of education, the attendance during the past twelve months being 86% instead of 96%'.

When John Henry Smith took up the Headship in April 1902 he also noted that attendance was poor, the children often staying at home to help in the garden. Harvest and hay-making times also saw attendances reduced. Adverse weather conditions - rain, thunderstorms and snow - prevented children from getting to school, as some lived two miles out of the village. At this time the only likely mode of transport was by foot. On occasions Mr Smith did not take the register in the afternoons 'to avoid having too low an attendance', so we assume that pupils sometimes did not return to school after lunch.

The new Act obliged Head teachers to report poor attendance to the Attendance Officer. A letter from the Managers was sent to parents in May 1902 to say that in future notes would be required to explain all absences. Attendance obviously improved in the following years as, in November 1910, the Attendance Banner[43] was awarded to the school for the best attendance for that month. In some weeks attendance reached 98%. In March 1940, the Education Office ordered that the figures for attendance should be cancelled for a week in February, as the low

---

[42] Boobery runs from Higher Town to Whitnage Road. The pump is still evident opposite Quay Head cottage, about 100m from the school.
[43] Awarded by DCC Attendance Committee each month.

attendance was due to the prevalence of epidemic sickness in the district. We must wonder to whom the Education Office was itself accountable.

Although much was made of children not attending school, time off was routinely given for many Saints' Days - generally a half-day holiday following a Church service in the morning. Sampford Fair meant a day's holiday for the children, many of whom participated or helped at the event. National events such as Empire Day;[44] the marriage, coronation or funeral of members of the Royal Family, and the end of a war, all earned another holiday, which could be anything from one day to one week. Activities for which the school was the venue, such as bazaars and use as a polling station, enforced a school closure and another holiday.

In March 1906 the Log Book records the children being allowed to witness the passing of elephants and camels belonging to a menagerie. As early as February 1913 the school 'timetable was interrupted by a photographer who took fifty-six exposures of the children in large and small groups', and in 1931 the excitement of another menagerie in the neighbourhood seemed to prevail upon the Managers, who gave the children a half-day's holiday.

Keeping Children Healthy

In the early 20th century there was much concern about the health of children nationally, especially among children from poor backgrounds, resulting in the passing of two more Acts of Parliament. The first, the Education (Provision of Meals) Act 1906 required LEAs to provide free meals to children whose parents could not afford to pay, instead of relying on voluntary donations. The second, The Education (Administrative Provisions) Act 1907, required LEAs to set up a Schools medical service to ensure that all children received a regular medical inspection and treatment for minor ailments. By 1937 this included inoculations against diphtheria. Regular visits by the school nurse, doctor, dentist and oculist were made and cases of ringworm, pediculosis and impetigo[45] were confirmed.

The 'Milk in Schools' scheme, which started in 1939, entitled twenty-two needy children to one third of a pint of milk per school day. The Headmaster, Mr Samuel, noted in the Log Book that 'some difficulty was experienced in getting the milk. Mr Wood of Morrell's Farm in Lower Town agreed to provide milk for this scheme on certain conditions which I [the Head] have endeavoured to meet'. The scheme ran from June until October that year, restarting in 1940; the cost per pint being 2½d reimbursed by DCC.

---

[44] Celebrated on May 24th, the birthday of Queen Victoria, which later became Commonwealth Day.
[45] Ringworm: a skin disease caused by fungi. Pediculosis: lice infesting the head or body. Impetigo: a bacterial skin infection that causes sores and blisters.

Over the years, there were several outbreaks of measles, chicken pox, diphtheria, whooping cough, influenza, German measles and scarlet fever, resulting in the school being closed for up to six weeks at any one time. As a precaution, if there was one incident of infection in a boy from St Boniface Home[46], then the remaining boys were kept away from school. In 1905 the Sanitary Authority even ordered the school to be closed for a week following severe cases of measles; this was then extended to five weeks in total.

Accidents Do Happen!

Possibly unaware of the consequences of his action, or maybe foolishly, in January 1907, the Headmaster, Mr Smith, went skating on the icy canal one Saturday. Unfortunately he managed to find a bit of thin ice under the bridge where he fell through and became immersed in six feet of water. It was just as well that, as pupils later recalled, he was an excellent swimmer! His accident and rescue by two villagers was not mentioned in the school Log Book, but featured in the Western Times of February 1907! Mr Voaden was also accident-prone. His collision on his motor-cycle at Battens Cross on the edge of the village resulted in a fractured leg, and two weeks absence from school.

Punishment

In 1911 Mr Smith started the only Punishment Book of which we are aware. This lists a variety of misdeeds: dishonesty, impudence, bullying, stealing, continued laziness, playing truant, talking in class, cheating, spoiling and wasting material, using bad language, and refusing to take punishment. Between one and six strokes of the cane were administered. The number of canings per year varied from twenty to forty-six between 1911 and 1937, after which it tailed off to fewer than seventeen per year, with some years having no entries at all (see Appendix 6).

Some of the more unusual 'crimes' included pupils leaving the premises without permission, and dishonesty in the Gardening Class, which resulted in a ban from swimming in the St Boniface bathing pool. The recorded misdemeanour of carelessness in the poultry run which caused a cockerel to be killed was probably an accident or at most an act of self-defence. Apparently, the cockerel was inclined to fly up at the boys working nearby and the boy concerned happened to have a spade in his hand. He batted the bird away, unfortunately causing its death from a broken neck.

---

[46] A children's home run by the Church of England Waifs and Strays Society from 1907 to 1952. It was situated in Lower Town, on land now occupied by the Court Way housing development.

The Punishment Book finished in 1984 prior to corporal punishment being outlawed in UK schools in 1987.

Physical Training

In the summer of 1906, the boys were taken to the village swimming pool[47] adjoining, and fed by, the canal. This happened twice a week instead of having drill[48]. Lessons were taken by the Headmaster, Mr Smith. Jack Scorse remembers that when any boy learned to swim across the pool, as nearly all of them did, Mr Smith gave him 'a tanner'[49]. This meant more to Jack than his adult monthly salary did many years later. No doggy-paddling was allowed: breaststroke only! In 1913 the girls were also allowed to use the pool, but separately from the boys, and after them. This was under the supervision of Mrs Smith, the Headmaster's wife, and did not finish until a quarter to five. No mixed swimming in those days! From 1910, the St Boniface boys were able to go swimming in their own pool, at the end of the day, under the supervision of their own masters.

By 1920, the boys had been given a football by Captain Young, the County organiser of physical training. The timetable was duly amended 'to enable boys to use it in turn'. Games were played on the St Boniface Home field after school, and a local football league was formed, playing on a Saturday. In the first game Sampford Peverell played against Bradninch, resulting in a 5-0 win for Sampford. Cricket matches were also played against other schools. The first Culm Valley Inter-Schools Sports took place in July 1933 at Uffculme. Seventy-eight children took part in a PT (Physical Training) and Folk Dancing display. This became an annual event, changing its format over the years. In 1940, the Log Book records Captain Young taking away the set of boxing gloves, which had been used by the Keep Fit Class of 1939. Was this because the Keep Fit class was no longer in existence, or were the precious gloves required elsewhere?

Pupil Numbers on the Roll

When school reopened in September 1907 after the summer holidays, the number of pupils showed a marked increase. The Church of England Waifs and Strays Society had opened a Children's Home, 'St Boniface' in the premises of the former East Devon County School on land which is now Court Way, next to the Globe Inn. Thirty-one 'Home' boys were admitted to the school bringing the number of pupils

---

[47] This pool may originally have been a tannery bath, near Buckland Bridge. The archway covering the culvert can still be seen from the canal path.
[48] Strict repetitive methodical group exercises.
[49] A tanner was colloquial for sixpence (6d), equivalent to over £1 today; well worth swimming for!

up to 145. The school obviously did not have enough room to accommodate all thirty-one newcomers, as in January 1908 eleven boys were transferred to Halberton school, only returning to Sampford Peverell school in September 1910 after the extension funded by Revd Philip Rossiter had been built. The number of Home boys tended to fluctuate throughout the years with several of the older ones being transferred to other Homes for vocational training or, as in May 1912, even being sent to Canada to learn farming processes there. By 1914 the school had obviously been reorganised sufficiently to accommodate 147 pupils, in its four classes. There was a marked drop in numbers between 1934 and 1936 owing to the transfer of Home boys of school age to another Home, reducing the total by 30%. By June 1937 the pupils numbered only 84, the lowest recorded for many years, as a result of the transfer of Home boys to another Church of England Home for vocational training. The numbers on the roll fluctuated considerably over the following years, with the the arrival and departure of evacuees during the Second World War and then the closure of St Boniface Home in 1952. This must have been an organisational nightmare for the Head and staff, with numbers varying from 100 to 211.[50]

The First World War

The First World War seems to have had very little effect on life in Sampford Peverell. The first mention of the war in the school Log Book was made on 20th November 1914, when permission was sought from the Education Committee to devote the first half of Sewing Time to work for the soldiers serving in Europe and elsewhere. Presumably this was granted as being a patriotic gesture. However, in July 1915 the application by the Attendance Sub Committee to close the school for the hay harvest was rejected 'as shortage of agricultural labour was not deemed to be exceptional in this parish'.

An entry in the Log Book in May 1917 refers to groups of children continuing to collect herbs on instruction from Tiverton. The herbs gathered were dandelions (the root), coltsfoot (the whole plant) and celandine (the leaves) but whether this was for the war effort or merely for home consumption we do not know.

Sewing, not just for soldiers, was clearly deemed to be a very important and necessary skill for girls at that time. The Log Book records extra afternoons being devoted to sewing as 'the girls are very behind hand with their needlework'. This could be partly due to the fact that between May 1915 and May 1916, eight different teachers were appointed to teach Standards I and II and Needlework. Perhaps it was one of these teachers who was given leave of absence to see her

---

[50] See Appendix 5, graph of numbers on the roll.

brother before his departure to the Front. He, however, was unable to get leave and the pair had to wait another three weeks before they were able to meet up. In January 1918 the teachers and children at the school donated £1 12s 6d to the Christmas fund for the Children of Blinded Soldiers.

The Log Book records the end of hostilities on 11th November 1918. 'Today came the news that fighting had ceased at 11 am, an armistice having been signed with Germany. After singing the National Anthem, the school was dismissed'. A day's holiday was granted. The children observed a two-minute silence on subsequent anniversaries at the request of King George V.

Rural Science

Lessons in gardening began in 1926 on a plot of land abutting the school and rented from the Rector, Revd J J Rees. Much of the preparation work was done by twenty of the older boys; making paths, preparing the ground, and creating a lawn on the slope. Manure came from the bucket lavatories and the fowl pens, with further nutrients from the compost heap. The boys were taught how to double dig, how to create a fine tilth and how to sow seeds, two at a time, along the length of the drill. Talks were given by outside speakers on the growing and propagation of fruits and vegetables. The children also visited the Rectory garden to learn about pruning and tree planting. Vic Maynard and Dennis Russell, pupils at the school during the war, have described how they were instructed in gardening, poultry keeping, beekeeping and butter making.[51] They recall that crops grown included apples, blackcurrants, raspberries, potatoes, carrots, parsnips, turnips, kidney beans, broad beans, peas, cabbages, leeks, onions, parsley and lavender. Potatoes were grown for school use; other produce was sold off to villagers. Timetables were often altered to ensure that the potato crop was harvested in optimum weather conditions, to avoid losses. Their recollection is that girls were involved in few of the activities because this was 'men's work only' in the 1940s. The older girls picked lavender, took it into class and split it into small bundles to be sold. Lessons in gardening were useful as all households had big gardens, and growing food was necessary for feeding large families.

One pupil recalls the importance Mr Samuel continued to give to this aspect of the curriculum following his appointment as Head in 1931. Mr Samuel even attended a three-month course on Rural Science at Seal Hayne College in Newton Abbot in summer 1939.

The school took possession of a new poultry shed in 1933; a grant of £8 was given by the County inspector to cover the cost of purchase and construction. The Head,

---

[51] Interviewed by Christine Mason April 2012.

Mr Samuel, recorded in the Log Book: 'A bold endeavour is made to introduce 'Poultry Keeping' as a subject on the curriculum, and three hens have been sitting some days'. The project was obviously successful. Devon County organiser Miss Cummins, and later Miss Lloyd, visited the school quite regularly over the course of the next six years to check the poultry and give lectures and demonstrations on how to kill, pluck, draw and dress fowl. An incubator was also trialled at the school, the senior class being given instruction over several mornings. The school kept thirty or forty chickens – Rhode Island Reds, Wyandottes, and Light Sussex, among other breeds. Some eggs were sold and some stored in isinglass for when the chickens went 'off lay'. Two boys were awarded prizes at the first of what became annual Poultry Shows. In 1937, the Log Book records the delivery of 96 day-old chicks, showing that poultry keeping was still thriving. Some former pupils recall that Mr Samuel himself taught the boys how to pluck, draw and dress a fowl, using his desk as a demonstration table, presumably in addition to the efforts of the County Advisors.

Beekeeping was added to the curriculum in 1937, with advisers coming into the school to give lectures on various aspects of the subject. A hive and bees were purchased on May 29th from a Mr Burgess of Exeter. Only a month later the queen flew off taking most of her workers in the swarm, and on 28 June the Log Book recorded that Mr Burgess called 'to rectify the hive by adding bees to those that remained'. He and Mr Samuels taught the boys how to make royal jelly to feed the

Poultry class, 1935, Revd Rees and Mr Samuel officiating

queen bee. They also learnt how to calm the swarm with smoke and how to use the separator machine to remove the honey from the comb. Honey was sold for a few pennies. Competitions in the art of beekeeping were arranged by the County inspector, with school teams competing for a Silver Cup. In 1940 the woodwork class contributed to the beekeeping project by making a full-size beehive, presumably for a new colony. There would have been no shortage of pollen in the well-stocked school garden and other gardens nearby.

A dairy course was started in March 1938 with the arrival of a mobile dairy installation. This plant (for butter making) was set up with the assistance of the senior pupils in the Carpentry Workshop, which shared a party wall with the outside toilets. The toilets faced the school playground, the workshop facing the gardens, which covered the area now used as school playing fields. Dairying proved to be a popular course, with twenty-five senior pupils attending. Norrish's Dairy in Chains Road[52] supplied the milk and Miss Bray and Miss Coleman came from the Devon County Dairy School to teach the boys the whole process of turning milk into butter and packing it ready for sale. There was equipment for eight or nine people to churn milk and pat butter. Butter churns came in different sizes so that smaller boys could also work them. At the end of the course, certificates were awarded for

DCCs Dairy School Van, early 1900s *Courtesy of Tiverton Museum of Mid Devon Life*

---

[52] Now the site of Home Orchard housing development.

The mobile dairy unit in operation at the school, 1938

proficiency and merit in dairying. Fifteen boys achieved First Class, six achieved Second Class, and the remaining four achieved Third Class. The following day, the plant was dismantled and taken away from the school.

During the Second World War, some fathers were away with the armed forces, whilst others, in 'reserved occupations' on the farms, were producing food which, because of the U-boat submarine blockade during the Battle of the Atlantic, was in desperately short supply; a slogan of the time issued by the government was to 'Dig for Victory', and the Sampford school children joined in with this. On the 8th of January 1940, bacon, butter and sugar were rationed. This was followed by meat, tea, jam, biscuits, breakfast cereals, cheese, eggs, lard, milk and canned fruit. At this time the national egg ration was one a week per person, although hen keepers were allowed a ration of chicken food. By the winter of 1940 enemy U-boat submarines were sinking supply ships three times faster than they could be built, and meat, rationed by price, was cut to a shilling's worth, about 1 lb (450 gm) per person per week.[53]

In response, the village established the Sampford Peverell Rabbit Club, not, as might occur today, to keep them as pets, but for essential food – to be eaten! By September 1942 fifteen scholars were enrolled in the club. Lectures on rabbit keeping were given at the St Boniface Home in the village.

---

[53] Review of The Taste of War, Lizzie Collingham in Mail on Line at http://www.dailymail.co.uk/home/books/article-1351152/Q-What-deadliest-weapon-World-War-II-A-Starvation-killed-20-million-people-THE-TASTE-OF-WAR-BY-LIZZIE-COLLINGHAM.html Accessed May 2012.

All Singing, All Dancing

Originally from Wales, Mr and Mrs Samuel were both talented muscians and were keen to impart their love of music to their charges. One pupil, Ruth Sharland, remembered how Mrs Samuel tested everyone to see if they could sing. Being too shy to sing alone, children went up two at a time to be tested. The school choir, with Mr Samuel as choirmaster and Mrs Samuel as pianist, was very successful at Devon music festivals. Throughout the 1930s the school choir gained many accolades. The boys' choir was awarded the Harper Shield, and the mixed choir was awarded the Seaton Shield. They also received shields for sight reading. Both choirs, plus the girls' choir, were invited to sing (with trophy winners from other schools) at the Civic Hall in Exeter. This was clearly a very special event in the life of the school, as the Log Book records that 'this concert will be broadcast'. The Managers often granted a half-day's holiday 'to celebrate the choirs' successes at music festivals'. Concerts were given to raise money for the choir transport fund, and the school repair fund.

In May 1939, the HMI report on music stated: 'The school excels in the teaching of music. The singing is much above the average for schools of this type and the children's attainment in the more theoretical branches is well advanced' The school choir was also the church choir, and children were expected to go to church to sing twice on Sundays as well as attending Sunday school in the afternoon. If you absented yourself on a Sunday, on Monday morning the Head would want to know why! The choir sang at the wedding of the new Rector, Revd Joseph G Brunskill to

Winners of the Devon Music Thompson Trophy, 1937

Dutch-themed School play, 1934, Mr and Mrs Samuel on right

Marion Chappell, in 1941. Plays, concerts, folk dancing, pantomimes and shows were put on by the children at various times of year. In 1933 the Log Book records that 'The scholars performed the operetta entitled "Cinderella", in three Acts. Children from Infant, Junior and Senior departments took part, there being about ninety performers. Costumes and scenery were prepared by the school needlework and handwork classes, and proved very effective. The acting and singing was excellent and reflects great credit on the staff'.

Ruth Sharland and Margaret Jefferies, interviewed in June 2007, remembered doing Welsh country dancing, performing in a village concert and then being asked to perform at other venues. The girls wore green dresses with flared skirts, decorated with yellow French knots around the hem, and white frilly hats or tall black Welsh hats made from cardboard. Other country dances performed included "The Sailor's Hornpipe" and "The Handkerchief Dance".

There is no doubt that Mr Samuel was an inspirational teacher, covering the usual 'three Rs'[54], gardening, animal husbandry and singing, in his curriculum. He was strict and believed in punishing pupils for any misdemeanours, as evidenced by some of his pupils and the Punishment Book. However, he also had a strong sense of community, ensuring the school played a prominent part at local events. For example, at the village Flower Show, the choirs and folk dancing groups performed, items of needlework were entered in competitions, and 'a stall was set up by the school, showing garden produce, poultry and eggs. One pupil gave a demonstration on trussing'.

[54] Reading, wRiting and aRithmetic.

The Fire of 1939

In March 1939 a row of three thatched cottages opposite the school caught fire. The "Express & Echo" newspaper reported that the children carried on calmly with their lessons.

> 'Wisps of smoke entered the school....and windows became hot. Mr Samuel allowed no measure of panic among his pupils, even though one boy knew his home was going up in flames. While the local fire brigade sprayed water at the school windows to prevent them breaking from the intense heat, Mr Samuel got the children singing to drown out the noise. He said that today the children were writing essays on the fire, describing the scene of ruin'.

The Second World War

In September 1939, on the first day back at school, instructions had been received from the Board of Education to close the school until further notice on account of the declaration of war. The Log Book notes that 'Scholars evacuated from London are expected to share our school building for the duration'. Preparations were made ready for their accommodation; workbenches were being taken outside to the outhouse, in order to accommodate more desks inside. A week later, the only evacuees in the village, numbering about ten, were those staying with friends. In 1940 many children were evacuated from cities considered to be likely targets of enemy bombing, such as London and, in the West Country, Plymouth[55], and some of the Londoners arrived in Sampford Peverell and joined our school. By June of that year, ninety-three evacuees from Edmonton, London, were admitted, with their three teachers: Miss Bradstrat, Miss Simpson and Miss Burton. Forty-six infants were accommodated in the village Memorial Hall[56] in two classes; thirty-six juniors were found space in the school, along with nine seniors who were amalgamated with the senior scholars. In early November 1940 the infants were moved to the Methodist vestry[57] as a temporary measure, since the Memorial Hall had been commandeered by the Military. Later the infants returned to the main school, and the juniors moved to the Methodist vestry, remaining there until the end of July 1942. The number on the roll increased to 211 in 1941 with seven staff, including the three teachers from Edmonton. By September 1944, only thirty-two evacuees remained, the others having returned to London over the intervening years. Their teacher, Miss Burton, stayed at the school for three years, returning to Edmonton in January 1944. A year later only five evacuees were left among the 110 children on roll.

---

[55] The city of Exeter was bombed in May 1942, but this is not mentioned in the School Log Book.
[56] The Memorial Hall in Lower Town was built in 1933 to commemorate those who died in the First World War.
[57] The Methodist vestry was a small room on the ground floor of the Methodist Chapel.

We know that many of the evacuees were accommodated in households without children, this being where there was most room for them. It must have been difficult for some 'foster parents' to keep their charges amused, but the school did its best to help out. The evacuees were allowed to use the school playground during weekends and holidays, except when the lavatories were being upgraded in 1941. The Log Book notes that in the summer of 1940, 'To occupy the evacuees during three of the five weeks' summer break, a holiday campaign was set up with the teachers helping on a rota basis'. A similar scheme was repeated during the Easter holidays, with walks and other recreational activities being arranged. In 1941, the Log Book records the children having picked one and a half hundredweight[58] of blackberries over the holidays. These were sold to the Women's Institute, who must have been very busy bottling fruit and making jam. The seniors visited hedgerows to collect rose hips (three-quarters of a hundredweight) which were sold to Messrs Carter and Son in Bristol, presumably for the production of rose hip syrup, given to babies and young children for its high vitamin C content.

Susan Hess, who researched the experiences of evacuees in Devon, interestingly argues that the acclimatisation of evacuated children was particularly successful in Devon, and that the drift back home was less than the national average. She also notes that local evidence suggests that contemporary national reports of impoverished, dirty and ill-mannered evacuees were frequently exaggerated, and that evacuation was actually central in accelerating post-war reform in education, child care and welfare.[59] Some children never returned to their original homes, but remained in Devon because their parents had moved here and decided to work in Devon; either because they could not settle back at home or because their families were broken as a result of death or divorce.[60] The young Eileen Parker arrived in the village aged 10 and became a pupil at the school, leaving and going back to Edmonton, London, at 14. Life had been hard for her mother so Eileen was needed to go to work and boost the family income. She worked in London for three years but then was ill. She returned to Devon to recover her health, living with the Hookways, the couple who had taken her in as an evacuee. Eileen remains here to this day, the only evacuee of her group to remain in Sampford Peverell.

The school authorities in London did provide some equipment to the Devonshire schools hosting their children, including such things as woodwork benches[61].

The school clearly tried to keep going with a normal routine throughout the war, and little is recorded in the Log Book of external events. However, it does record

---

[58] One hundredweight (cwt) is equivalent to 45.36 kg.
[59] Hess S J (2006) "Civilian Evacuation to Devon in the Second World War" thesis for the degree of Doctor of Philosophy in History, University of Exeter. P. 388.
[60] Hess S J (ibid.) p. 182.
[61] A School Log Book note in late 1944 records that a London County Council van removed eight of the woodwork benches to an Exeter depot for return to the south London school *Charlton*.

parents being given a demonstration on the use of 'gas helmets' by the school nurse in October 1939, and the taking over of the school garden for the duration of the war. The planting of vegetables took priority over some other subjects in the curriculum. Another recorded effect of the War on the school was that at Whitsun in May 1940 the week's half term holiday was cut short. The school was reopened after just one day's holiday 'by request from the Board of Education due to the war emergency', presumably to keep the children occupied and away from the concerns of the population, for this was the desperate time when some 330,000 British and Allied soldiers were evacuated from the beaches of Dunkirk. Another entry, in 1941, records a special effort in War Savings[62] collection, made for War Weapons Week.[63] £8 5s[64] was realised and fifteen certificates were awarded to the keen savers.

School interior, 1940s

---

[62] A national savings scheme encouraging children in schools and employees in workplaces to deposit small amounts regularly. Attractive posters were part of the campaign, which swelled the Treasury coffers.
[63] Instigated as a result of the depletion of equipment and arms after the allied withdrawal from Europe via Dunkirk, to re-equip the army in the face of threatened German invasion, and to deter people from withdrawing savings, which would have created an economic crisis.
[64] Equivalent to almost £300 today.

During the Second World War a larger plot of land was added to the garden and fenced off for additional use. Gardening lessons must have continued throughout, as a brief note in the Log Book in April 1943 quotes 'Extra lessons given this week in gardening on account of fine weather and inadequate staffing'. That's one way of sorting a staff shortage!

The war-time changes persisted for several years after the advent of peace, and it was not until July 1949 that the poultry sheds were removed, and a decision made to turn the school garden into a playing field. However, some activities continued, and the log book records that in the summer of 1953 the school won 'again' the Furze cup for beekeeping, sadly losing it the following year to South Molton County Primary school. The war changed social attitudes to a great degree, and even greater emphasis was put upon the health and education of the nation's children.

The school building, 1960s

Chapter V

The Church of England Primary School: 1944 to 2000

This chapter considers the next six decades of the school's history. It was a period of great change: from a time when the (locally produced) milk might be delivered by horse and trap; the fields were ploughed by horse power, and the village forge had regular custom; to classrooms full of computers connected to the World Wide Web; from a very rural economy to a world where children may arrive at school by car. The concerns over children's health shifted from the rationing of food and malnutrition among evacuees, to problems with obesity. Tuberculosis and other infectious diseases were then not uncommon but, in the present-day village, TB is unknown, and the others rare.

The children's health

References to the children's health occur occasionally in the records of these years, although rarely mentioning actual disease, even among the evacuees. In January 1943 a boy, at the St Boniface home rather than at the primary school, developed typhoid, a bacterial disease characterised by diarrhoea, fever and headache, which can be fatal. However, by the mid twentieth century the way in which it arose (from contaminated water) was well understood, and in this case it was traced to a stream used as an open sewer. Vaccination against the disease had been introduced at the beginning of the century, and several of the Sampford Peverell schoolchildren subsequently visited the doctor to be vaccinated.

In December 1943 and the following January, thirty-five of the local children were vaccinated against diphtheria. At the time this disease was much feared; victims have a high fever and sore throat, and a membrane forms across the throat thick enough to impede breathing. In England and Wales in 1940 there were 40,000 cases, including 2,500 children, and around 2,400 people died of the disease. Vaccination against the disease was introduced in 1940, following a decision by the Ministry of Health to provide central funding, but some local authorities were slow to act on this, and by the end of 1942 only one third of English children had been fully vaccinated[65]. The school log book notes that the evacuee children were not immunised when the local children were. No reason is given but one may

---

[65] Mortimer P (2010) Diphtheria and the origins of the UK childhood immunization problem. *Microbiology Today*, February 2010, and Escola J et al. (1998) Resurgent diphtheria – are we safe? *British Medical Bulletin*, 54, 3, 636-645.

guess that the County Council would pay only for Devon children.

In 1906 the Education (Provision of Meals) Act had allowed, but not required, schools to provide meals for pupils, but Local Education Authorities were slow to respond, and under the 1944 Education Act the provision of school meals and milk became a statutory responsibility[66]. In 1953 a 'scullery' (more accurately a kitchen) was added to the school buildings. Unfortunately this was described a year later, following a visit by the County Medical Officer, as being 'not large enough'; despite this, meals continued to be cooked and served from this tiny kitchen to the present day.

Changing attitudes to care of the children's health is shown in several ways. In 1941 the 'County Psychologist' was called in to see a child whose bad record of thieving had been recorded in the Punishment Book. So-called 'medical milk' had been supplied to some children as a provision of the 1907 Education Act, and in 1944 the log book records that some of the Sampford children were in receipt of it. By 1948 milk, pasteurised to control milk-borne disease, was supplied to the school through the Co-operative Wholesale Society, Wellington.

Following the introduction of the National Health Service in 1948, there were regular tests for tuberculosis (TB) and for possible eye problems; heads were inspected for lice; there were dental inspections and thorough medical inspections. Tuberculosis was a matter of great concern after the war: in 1950, 50,000 cases occurred, leading to a programme of mass radiography[67], focussing on chest X-rays, as this is the commonest site of infection of this mycobacterial disease. In January 1954 the Sampford children underwent the 'jelly test' for TB[68], to which twenty-three of them reacted positively. Within a few days they were sent to a mass radiography unit operating in the neighbouring village of Uffculme. The results of this test are not recorded, but testing for TB was still being performed on the schoolchildren in 1966. The respiratory health of the children was a concern in other ways, for, as late as the spring of 1967, members of the top class were sent home in the afternoon, to prevent their breathing 'noxious fumes' emitted by the coke stove still used to heat their classroom. A similar event occurred in 1991, when a surprising number of children had to be sent home with headaches over several weeks: fortunately one teacher, Mrs Bond, acted on this, and the cause was traced to a leaking gas heater. Infections inevitably occurred from time to time: in 1971 the

---

[66] Gillard D (2003) *Food for Thought: child nutrition, the school dinner and the food industry* at www.educationengland.org.uk/articles/22food.html. Accessed March 2013.

[67] Health Protection Agency, at http://www.hpa.org.uk/web/HPAweb&HPAwebStandard/HPAweb-C/1214808551403. Accessed July 2012.

[68] In this test a small area of the back was lightly abraded with fine sandpaper, and a small quantity of tuberculin jelly applied; the area was then covered in a plaster. This was removed after 48 hours, and the test site examined and scored on the following day. See http://www.ncbi.nlm.nih.gov/pmc/articles/PMC2038191/?page=1. Accessed July 2012.

Log Book records that the Headmaster Mr Vickery, his wife the school secretary, Mrs Connah the infant teacher, and forty-five children were absent owing to a sudden and violent attack of 'some unspeakable virus of the digestive system'.

By 1996 the problems of handicapped children were being recognised, and a ramp was installed to facilitate wheelchair access - a means of welcoming those less physically able.

Early in 1953 a Miss Chetham visited the school showing PE (physical education) films and advising the children on how to dress for PE. Physical activity was always an important part of the school day, and a new swimming pool measuring 16' by 32' was erected beside the playground in the summer of 1966. This was replaced, in 1990, at a cost of about £8,000. Members of the Parent Teacher Friends Association (PTFA) not only raised much of the necessary funds, but voluntarily provided the labour also. Despite subsequently requiring two new liners, the pool remains in use by the school today. The children continued to visit other schools to play inter-school football and netball matches, as well as taking on new activities, such as the Exmoor Challenge.[69]

Towards the end of the twentieth century health concerns were equally serious, but changed in nature, for the School Log Book for January 1996 records that the teachers had an 'inset day' or 'in-service training day', instituted by the 1988 Education Reform Act. On this occasion the teachers attended a drug awareness course – for teachers of primary school children!

Changes in education

Education at the school has changed considerably over the years, as earlier chapters have shown. A highly important change occurred in 1944 with the introduction of a new Act of Parliament (called the Butler Act, after its promoter Mr R A Butler[70]). In response, most Local Education Authorities (LEAs) aimed to establish three main 'streams' or categories of school - grammar, secondary modern and technical - which had been recommended in a Report by Sir William Spens in 1938. Children would be allocated to one of these categories on the basis of an examination at the age of 11, known as the 'Eleven plus'. This was intended to provide equal opportunities for children of all backgrounds. Regular medical inspection of children was compulsory under the Act. In furtherance of the children's health, the LEA was to provide milk, meals and 'other refreshment'.

---

[69] A 16 mile hike on an unmarked route over Exmoor, in teams of four, requiring map reading and compass skills.

[70] Richard Austen Butler (always known as RAB) was responsible for the 1944 Education Act that created the pattern for post-war secondary schooling in Britain. He was a key figure in the Conservative Party in the 1950s.

Class photo, 1953

School photo, 1954

The Church of England Primary School: 1944 - 2000

Middle and Upper classes, 1955
Back row: Audrey Williams, Sylvia Wright, Wendy Burston, Francis Turner, Susan Grant
Next row: Molly Broomfield, Christine Turner, Glynis Passmore, Dawn Vickery, David Vickery (Headmaster), Janet Saunders, Brenda Rowe, Mary Goffin, Marion Brealy. Next row: David King, Derrick Broomfield, David Stone(?), Edward Bennett, Ronald Bennett, Darrel Burston, Colin Disney
Front row: Roger Workman, Alan Perkins, David Sharland, Martin Coleman, Roger Broomfield

Class photo, 1961
Back row: Stephen White, Len Sharland, Sheila Moon, Graham Howe, Denise Sharland, Christine Holly, Phillip Evett, Stuart Redwood, Ann King
Front row: Caroline Vickery, Karen Maynard, David Parkhouse, Nick Richards, (?) Prescott, Jenifer Disney, Stephen Parkhouse, Gordon Brealy, David Wright, Lisa (?) Russell

The changes were reflected early at Sampford Peverell School. In the spring of 1946, three children were successful at the Grammar School entrance examination (perhaps to Tiverton Grammar School). A year after these three 'successes' the Log Book records (in the terminology of the time) that 'All 11+ scholars on 1/1/47 who are not 14 yrs on April 1st, will, on April 21st attend Heathcoat [Secondary Modern] school in compliance with the reorganisation scheme.'[71]

By the 1960s many LEAs were establishing 'comprehensive' schools which catered for all abilities, but they modelled themselves in their early years on the traditional ethos of the grammar school. In June 1966 the Sampford Headmaster, David Vickery, attended a Heads' Conference to discuss their introduction. More changes were to be introduced following the 1964 Education Act, and the push to raise the school leaving age from 15 to 16 by 1973[72]. As part of this process, the Labour government in 1965 encouraged the provision of 'middle schools', and in February 1971 the Headmaster attended a meeting at County Hall about forming them in Devon. In the mid-1970s a fully comprehensive system started in Tiverton. Pupils attended First Schools from 5 – 9 years old; Middle Schools from 9 – 13 and a comprehensive school, with the name 'Tiverton School', from 13 – 18 years. This change affected Sampford only to some extent: since Tiverton Grammar School by then no longer existed, all the 11 year olds went instead to Uffculme Comprehensive.

In 1988 the government introduced the 'Education Reform Act' - legislation of major importance, and the most significant since the 1944 Act. However, there is remarkably little reference to it in the school's Log Books. This Act specified a 'basic curriculum' to be taught in all maintained schools (i.e. maintained by the Local Authority), consisting of religious education and the National Curriculum. The National Curriculum itself would set out attainment targets - the knowledge, skills and understanding which children would be expected to have by the end of each 'key stage'; the 'programmes of study' to be taught at each key stage; and the arrangements for assessing pupils at the end of each key stage. The Act was very prescriptive, defining 'core subjects' (mathematics, science and English, or Welsh in Welsh schools) and 'foundation subjects' (history, geography, technology, music, art and physical education; with a foreign language in later stages).

Certain 'key stages' were defined, with testing to be carried out at the ages of 7, 11, 14, and 16 years. (The latter are referred to as Standard Attainment Tests, or SATS).

---

[71] The personal experience of the author of this chapter was to have been taken out of the class at the age of eleven plus, with a few others, and crammed with past exam papers from the local grammar school. This was a life-changing experience for those on both sides of the divide.
[72] UK Middle Schools website and map at https://sites.google.com/site/middleschools/history/middle-schools-in-england. Accessed September 2012.

The Church of England Primary School: 1944 - 2000

The changes were not universally popular and were labelled 'unfair and unworkable' by many primary school teachers.[73] The Sampford school Log Books note that an evening meeting was held with parents in November 1989 to explain the new provisions. However, the school appears simply to have got on with teaching; there are only occasional references in the Log Books to the SATS test being taken.

The National Curriculum gave teachers a clear framework for teaching, with numerous training sessions delivered by an increased number of County Advisers, along with extra courses organised through the Teachers' Centre in Tiverton. The teachers of all the local schools met to plan the best way to deliver the new curriculum. This sharing of ideas and expertise was both stimulating and beneficial to teachers, and consequently to pupils.

However, there were drawbacks; for example, certain periods of history were 'in' and other periods were now 'out'. So Romans and Tudors and Victorians were to be taught, but Medieval England and Georgians were not! The consequence of this was that every child in the country would grow up knowing lots about Tudors, but nothing about their predecessors. This had a knock-on effect for suitable places for school visits, and of course on resources. Every possible school visit venue

Greek play, circa 1995 *Photo: Gill Bowers*

[73] At https://www.guardian.co.uk/education/2004/aug/24/schools.sats. Accessed July 2012.

had to display the 'Attainment Targets' that could be covered in their location; the race was on to prove their site as worthy of a visit. A further drawback to this was that when every school ordered the same resources from the Library Resources Centre at the same time, there were not enough to go round. Probably this was a headache for the staff at the Centre, too!

Another review of the curriculum in 1999 emphasised the importance of outdoor experiences for Foundation Stage[74] children. An outside play area was created through the hard work and dedication of members of the Parent-Teachers-Friends-Association (PTFA, formerly the Parents Teachers Association or PTA, see page 88). The nation was concerned that children had become too inclined to stay indoors and watch television.

The weather is always with us

Inclement weather continued to feature often in the school records, sometimes resulting in closure of the school, either because of difficulty in reaching the school, or because lavatories were frozen. During the very severe winter of 1946-1947, the school closed from January 30th to February 5th, but even in early March the lavatories were unusable. On the 5th March only six scholars had been able to navigate the severely icy roads, leading to closure for another three days. It closed again on February 28th 1955, as all the lavatories were again frozen, but, battling on, it re-opened the next day as one toilet at least could be used. The winter of 1962 to 1963 was one of the worst to affect England for centuries, being both very cold, and very prolonged - from December to March. According to the Log Book for 8th January, School re-opened *(after the Christmas holiday)*, despite the fact that there was a depth of 23 ins of snow surrounding the School and playground. However, by January 14th it closed again as not only the lavatories but the pipes supplying them were frozen solid. Later, even the main supply to the school froze, and the school remained closed for four weeks until February 8th.

The summer of 1976, in contrast, was noted as being 'exceptionally hot indeed', and that 'We are enduring the longest drought for over 500 years'. The rivers were 'mere trickles' and water rationing had been introduced. In January 1990, wind was the problem, for ridge tiles and slates crashed down, smashing windows in the school cook's car. The children were taken to the main hall, it being the safest place, and the Deputy Head Miss Reynolds organised singing and action songs. By use of the school's single telephone, certain parents were contacted who, each in turn, according to a pre-arranged system, informed others and by 2.30 pm, when all the children had been collected, the school closed.

---

[74] Pupils aged 4 and 5 in schools.

Celebrating the centenary of the school

In 1974 the School celebrated the fact that it had been in existence for one hundred years. The Log Book contains a detailed account of the event, written by the Headmaster David Vickery, and is here given in full.

'The school celebrated its centenary with a Thanksgiving service held in the church, at which the newly-installed Lord Bishop of Exeter (Eric Mercer) gave the address. This address was to the children and was very moving in its simplicity and impact. After the service, which was preceded and followed by a peal of bells, the invited guests were entertained to sherry by the Rector at the rectory. Luncheon followed at the school. Sixteen sat down to the meal. They were: Mr A. K. Mowll, Area Education Officer, Mrs Clapshaw[75], Mrs Jean Bonnard, H.M.I. The Rector of the parish Revd A.B. Nelson and Mrs Nelson, the Headmaster and Mrs Vickery, the teaching staff- Mrs Kulczyk, Mrs Connah, Mrs Bridel and Mrs Dixon, Mrs Newton, Preb [Prebendary] Sampson Director of R.I.[Religious Instruction] in the diocese, Mr and Mrs Paul Matthews from Blundell's and Mr Gerry Wilson-Smith, official photographer. After lunch, the guests were entertained to coffee at High Cross House by Mr and Mrs Kulczyk. In the afternoon other guests joined the platform party. They were, Mr A.E. Wood, Headmaster of Uffculme school, Miss E. Rogers (ex staff) Headmistress of Heathcoat Infants School Tiverton, Miss E.D. Mitchell (ex staff), Mr C. Goffin Chairman of the Parish Council, Mr D. Lister President of the P.T.A, The school managers- Dr J.W. Graves-Morris, Mr H.J. Perry, Mr K. Keitch and Mrs Lister, the two church wardens, Col C.B. Church and Mrs Church and Mr Ken Wright and Miss Joan Carter, Headmistress of Uplowman School.

Procession to Church, Centenary celebration 11 July 1974
Photo: Jenny Parsons

'Certificates were awarded to the children for swimming, athletics and academic success. Also each child attending the school was presented with a specially struck commemorative mug and the managers presented a new sports shield to the school. The

---

[75] Mrs Rita Clapshaw was the daughter of the former Headmaster, Mr Samuel. In 1974 she was Deputy Head of the Clyst Vale Community College, Broadclyst, some ten miles from Sampford Peverell.

occasion was also marked by the institution of a special Centenary booklet, edited by Mrs Lister. Copies of the thanksgiving service sheet, the afternoon's programme and the Centenary Booklet should all be found at the back of the log book. After the presentations, guests and parents inspected the many exhibitions and displays of old photographs and pictures of the village and members of Sampford Peverell families and the many old artefacts and documents and items of Victoriana. Tea was served by members of the P.T.A. I must not omit to add that I, my staff and most of the children were clothed in the garb of a century ago for the occasion.

'Altogether, it was a very happy and successful day and one which I hope will be memorable for the children who were present. Perhaps some of them will be in this locality when the school - if it still exists - celebrates its one hundred and fiftieth birthday [in 2024]. Perhaps one of them may then read this.'

Wider activities

As in previous years, church activities, and their relevance to the wider world, were an important part of the school's life. So, on Wednesday June 6th 1944, that morning's session ended at 11.45 am 'to enable staff and children to attend service at the Parish church at 12 pm [noon], a service of intercession for the invasion of Europe which commenced at dawn today'. A day's holiday was granted in November 1944 'to celebrate induction & institution of Revd M E Coyle to the incumbency of S.P.'

In April 1947 the school was closed on account of both Sampford Fair and the Silver Wedding Anniversary of King George VI and Queen Elizabeth[76]. The school closed again that October for Bampton Fair, about nine miles away. In May 1953 the local Brownies had collected £8 10s 0d for the erection of a flagstaff to commemorate the Coronation year; it was to be erected by the builders then working on the new scullery. The doings of royalty have been consistently celebrated and, for the Coronation itself in June, the school had a week's holiday; the flagstaff being then officially presented to the school. However, when the Queen's sister, Princess Margaret, married a commoner, Mr Anthony Armstrong Jones, they had just one day's holiday. The whole school assembled in 1969 to watch on television the investiture of Prince Charles as Prince of Wales, and three years later there was a day off on the occasion of the Queen's Silver Wedding Anniversary. In 1977, for the Queen's Silver Jubilee, the school was decorated with a large Union Jack, there was a day off, and each child received a commemorative 'Silver Jubilee Crown' (a coin with a face value of five shillings). However, the children did their bit too, when a choir of twenty-four children entertained senior citizens of the village at a Jubilee Tea in the village Memorial Hall.

---

[76] The first charter to hold a fair in Sampford Peverell, was granted in 1335. The last fair was held circa 1950.

School Christmas party, 1981

External visits were made often. In July 1954 most of the children journeyed to Plymouth, going over Dartmoor and returning by the coast road. The following year the journey by coach was northwards to Lynton and Lynmouth, Porlock and Dunster, a route which would have taken them down the 1 in 4 hill into Porlock. By the late 1960s the visits were more adventurous. In September 1967 the Headmaster took twenty-three of the older children to London on an excursion train and, in what must have been a whirl, they visited the Tower of London, the Natural History and Science museums and 'other places of interest in the city', and also watched the changing of the guard at Buckingham Palace. Visits also became longer: in the summer of 1988 twenty-two children and six adults went to the Start Bay Residential Centre[77] for a four-day visit. These visits continued, with both Start Bay and Pixie's Holt on Dartmoor being favourite Devon centres for the residential experience, which became a statutory requirement under the National Curriculum, for pupils of Year 6 aged 10-11.

---

[77] The Centre is based in a converted Victorian school, with accommodation, now run by the Field Studies Council.

During Mr Rumsey's tenure as Headmaster (1985-2000), instruction about the railways was not neglected. Upon the opening of Tiverton Parkway Station, on 12 May 1986, the whole school walked to the Station to attend the opening ceremony. On another occasion, being the 150th anniversary of the Bristol and Exeter Railway, a special event was to take place at St David's Station, Exeter. A steam engine, en route to this event, was due to stop at Tiverton Parkway, and all the schoolchildren walked down to the Station to see it. However, the train went through earlier than scheduled, and without stopping! On the following day, in order to compensate the children for their disappointment at having missed the spectacle, the organisers provided free places on a special excursion coach behind the returning steam train.

The Parent-Teacher Association (PTA) is first mentioned as supporters of the school in 1965, when the Association paid for sixty children to visit the Tiverton Signpost Club's pantomime 'The Old Woman who Lived in a Shoe'. In 1987 the emergence of relatively inexpensive computers led the PTA, by now with a significant role in fund-raising, to organise a Christmas Bazaar which raised £281: a year later a sponsored walk along part of the towpath of the Grand Western Canal (which runs through the village) raised over £400 'towards buying a second computer'. Other charities supported by the school included, in 1989, an appeal for funds to support

Nativity play, 1984

the country of Kampuchea; £184 was raised[78]. A most surprising act of charity occurred shortly before Christmas 1992, when the school closed early in order to deliver about fifty parcels for 'underprivileged children who live in Tiverton'.

At the end of the twentieth century, life in Sampford Peverell Primary School continued much as it had for the preceding years since its establishment by the Revd Boulton. There was considerable care for the children's health, and they were taught to look outwards, not just to their local farms but to the world environment. To mark the coming Millennium, a Time Capsule was buried in the School's 'Environmental Area' on July 21st 1999 (the 125th anniversary of the building of

Burial of the Time Capsule, 1999, presided over by the Right Revd Richard Hawkins, Bishop of Crediton, and Michael Rumsey

the school on its present site). Educational partnerships were set up with Poland and Germany, with children travelling to meet their European counterparts. With the support of the Sampford Peverell and District Twinning Association, the school hosted children from Notre Dame de Courson in May 1999, and pupils of Years 5 and 6 paid a return visit to Normandy the following year. In 2003, a Japanese intern spent nine months in the school, sharing the culture of her homeland with the children, culminating in 'Japanese Days' in which the whole school participated.

---

[78] The invasion of Kampuchea by Vietnamese forces was an extension of the bitter wars in Vietnam in the 1970s and 1980s. See http://en.wikipedia.org/wiki/Cambodia%E2%80%93Vietnamese-War. Accessed July 2012.

Japanese day 2003 *Photo: Dixon Cowan*

With the arrival on the staff of Miss Wendy Reynolds in 1992, the musical life of the school underwent something of a renaissance, with the formation of an orchestra and several choirs. The 'Sampford Peverell Young Singers' (SPYS) came first, quickly followed by even younger voices (SPYLETS). There were frequent concerts and full-scale productions, such as 'Joseph and his Amazing Technicolor Dreamcoat' - not only at the School and in the village hall but, increasingly, further afield. Each year, Miss Reynolds organised a Summer Music School which was held during the first week of the school holidays and was attended by children from all over the Culm Valley.

To mark the Millennium, Miss Reynolds successfully applied for a National Lottery grant, which enabled her to commission and stage a musical production depicting the history of the village in words and music. Over 100 residents took part in 'The Sampford Story', including 55 children from the School. The Sampford Peverell Memorial Hall was sold out for 5 performances in July 1999 and the show went 'on tour' (as far as Tiverton!) 4 months later, where the New Hall was filled to capacity for two nights.

It was Miss Reynolds' success in reviving the musical life of the School (and of the village) that led to her being nominated for a National Teaching Award in 2000. She was the South West Regional winner in the category 'Working with Parents and the Community in a Primary School' and was presented with a handsome trophy (known as a 'Plato') to keep and – perhaps more importantly – a cheque made payable to Sampford Peverell Primary School for £3500!

The School continued to provide a rounded education, augmenting the curriculum with science and art days, Healthy Fortnights and Safety Fortnights. Visitors to the school included police officers, artists, nurses, potters, scientists and travelling theatre groups as well as the weekly visit from the incumbent rector for the daily act of worship. Fund raising events took place, such as 'Jeans for Genes' (for Great Ormond Street Children's Hospital). Pancake Day was still celebrated. Remembrance Day and National Poetry Day enlarged their horizons yet further. The teachers continued to provide for their charges, but more Education Acts were to come (see Chapter VII).

The School Bank

Just over 100 years since the unsuccessful attempt to start a 'Penny Bank' in the School (see Chapter II), another means of encouraging the children to save was introduced. In 1985, under the Headship of Michael Rumsey, and with assistance from the Tiverton branch of the Midland Bank, a bank was established in the school. This was very unusual in a primary school, and the aim was to 'get them

School Bank, 1986

into the saving habit'. *The Tiverton Gazette* reported that senior pupils were to act as cashiers and ledger clerks, to be responsible for 'looking after the needs of their clients'. The pupils had to amass a saving of £10 (now equal to about £25), when they would be presented with 'a sports file, an action file, an Oxford Dictionary and stationery'. The savings would also then begin to accumulate interest. At the opening ceremony, the manager of the Midland Bank also presented Mr Rumsey with a cheque for the school of £100.

Expansion of the School

As with many other Victorian schools of Devon, by the mid 20th Century the original buildings no longer provided for the demands of the curriculum. Sadly the sloping site has not lent itself to the provision of permanent new, light and airy classrooms, as has happened in other local schools. Instead, a proliferation of 'Portacabins' mushroomed around the old Victorian building.

The first of these so-called 'temporary' classrooms, affectionately known as 'Devon Ladies', was erected on a solid brick foundation in the 1960s so that the infants could have their own classroom space, leaving the older pupils free to study in the quiet of the main building. On September 11th 1967 a new temporary classroom was erected behind the main hall for the infants' class. The lower junior class moved into the room previously occupied by the infants and that room was used as staff room, secretary's room and Medical Inspection room. In the early 1980s a further temporary classroom, surplus to requirements at Tiverton School, was located at the back of the car park area when pupil numbers rose above 100 (justifying the need for a fourth classroom along with the appointment of a Deputy Head.)

In the 1990s another temporary classroom, beside the swimming pool, freed up the hall for indoor PE lessons, music and drama, as well as for eating school dinners and packed lunches. No longer did the oldest pupils have to clear their desks fifteen minutes before lunch in order for the midday meal to be served.

Delivery of a temporary classroom, 1990s

The Church of England Primary School: 1944 - 2000

The exterior of the main building, here seen in 1999, has changed little since 1909

Photo: Jenny Holley

The school premises continued to expand into the twenty-first century. A smaller Portacabin arrived in 2002, to be the Head Teacher's office, when the balance of the Head's role moved from teaching to administration.

The influence of the World Wide Web would not pass by our small village. In 2003 there was just a single computer in the corner of each classroom, for which pupils had to wait their turn, but that year extra rooms were created upstairs in the Victorian roof space. These included an Information Technology or IT suite, allowing whole-class teaching of IT skills, plus the Head's office and a staff room. Staff numbers had grown, with as many non-teaching staff (classroom assistants, mealtime assistants and administrative staff) as teachers. At last there was a dedicated room for the staff; a mere corner of the library to make tea had been grossly inadequate. In addition, by 2005, the classrooms had interactive whiteboards[79] and every teacher his or her own laptop. In 2006 a double classroom replaced the dilapidated classroom at the back of the car park. This allowed the only classroom remaining inside the original school building to be reused as the school office. Formerly the school had employed just one part-time secretary, but now an office was needed to house three part-time administrators.

---

[79] A wall mounted board connected to a computer and projector, allowing the computer's desktop to become interactive by pupils using a pen or stylus to move images, add text etc.

Rear extension of the Methodist Chapel, where the Sunday School was held   Photo: Dixon Cowan

Chapter VI

Other Schools

Sunday Schools

Whilst there is no mention in the records of Sunday Schools before 1839, it is likely that they had been in existence for quite some time, perhaps several decades or more. Nowadays kept in the Church bell-tower, are two pairs of painted boards, which may have been used for Sunday School tuition: the first pair gives the Creed and the Lord's Prayer, and is dated 1824, having been provided by the Churchwardens; the second pair sets out the ten commandments, and is undated. The

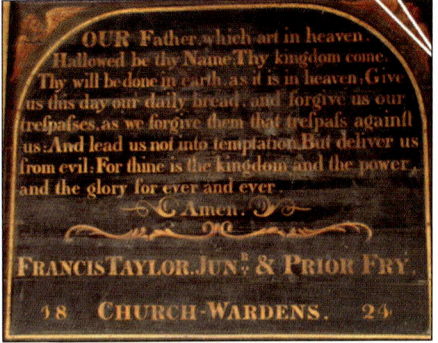

Lord's Prayer board, 1824   Photo: Peter Bowers

first record of a Sunday School for children of the Wesleyan Church appears in the Western Times dated 9 November 1839. The Centenary of Methodism provided the occasion for a roast beef and plum pudding dinner, attended by upwards of 250 individuals, including 117 children of the Wesleyan Sunday School. The Exeter and Plymouth Gazette of 18 April 1840 records, upon the occasion of laying the first stone for the new parsonage house, that 'The Revd Edward Pidsley regaled the children of the Sunday Schools, nearly ninety in number, with a sumptuous dinner of roast beef and plum pudding, and afterwards with tea, provided for them at the expense of the worthy Rector'. We can, therefore, conclude that by 1840 both 'Church and Chapel' had their own Sunday Schools.

A bizarre incident was reported in the Western Times on 3 June 1843 concerning 'the Schoolmaster of the Church Sunday School in Sampford Peverell' [his name is unknown]. He had been summoned before Tiverton Magistrates for

> 'An unprovoked assault on a young man called Creed. It appears a short time since Creed was quietly walking up the street, when the wielder of the birch, being pot valiant [80], took Creed by the collar, and endeavoured to hold him fast until some navvies should arrive and give the offending man a sound flogging'.

---

[80] Bold or courageous whilst under the influence of alcohol.

The schoolmaster was found guilty, reprimanded, fined one shilling, bound over to keep the peace for a year and had to pay the expenses which amounted to thirty shillings. Most unusually, his name does not appear in the newspaper article, so he was spared wider publicity.

The 1851 Religious Census shows that the Wesleyan Sunday School was still thriving: sixty attended in the morning and thirty in the evening. This exceeded the attendance at the Anglican Sunday School, which was recorded as twenty-five in the morning and twenty-five in the afternoon on the same date. Such was the attendance at the Wesleyan Sunday School that a two-storey schoolroom was added to the Chapel at some time before 1870. *[For more information about the Wesleyan Chapel, see the Society's publication "Sampford Peverell: The Village, Church, Chapels and Rectories"]*

It would seem that the Anglican Sunday School did not fare so well during the late 1850s and the 1860s, according to a letter written by J Mardon to the Western Times in 1907. In this he recalled that he had known the Wesleyan Sunday School from 1859 and for many years had been a teacher there, at which time the attendance numbered 140 children. He also wrote that there was no Sunday School at the Church until Mrs Hill arrived [which, by reference to the Land Tax Returns, was in 1868] and that she was the means of starting one. Perhaps the advent of the National School and Mr Chave's Academy in the 1850s had temporarily reduced the demand for Anglican Sunday School education, which had previously been so well supported.

The two Sunday Schools were still in operation in 1907, when the Sampford Peverell Charitable Trust was set up to award prizes to children at the school, as discussed in Chapter IV. By this time, there were 106 pupils attending the Church of England Primary School, of whom forty-eight were connected with the Wesleyan Sunday School. Ron Venner, a lifelong resident of Halberton, recalls that, as a boy in the 1940s, Sundays would be spent attending the Halberton Wesleyan Chapel service in the morning, and then the Sampford Peverell Wesleyan Sunday School in the afternoon. At that time, the Sunday School was well-attended and run by a Miss Thomas. In addition to the schooling on Sundays, Ron recalls that there was an annual outing, for example to the seaside, and a concert in which all the pupils were encouraged to participate.

The Wesleyan Sunday School finally closed in the early 1990s, due to falling attendance. At around the same time the Anglican Sunday School was experiencing a revival, with the children being taught in the Vestry during the Sunday service. However, the tide of change meant that the demand for Sunday-schooling continued to diminish and by the early years of the new millennium it finally ceased to be available in either village Church.

Mrs Wallington's School

During the 19th and the early part of the 20th centuries, the education provided for girls at the National School (subsequently the Church of England Primary School) was rudimentary, with a heavy bias towards sewing and domestic skills. For parents who wanted rather more for their daughters and were prepared to pay for it, alternatives had been available in the village, firstly at Turberfield School and later on at the East Devon County School. After the closure of the latter in 1907, no such alternative existed until Mrs Bright Wallington established a girls' boarding school at her home in Morrells House, Lower Town, in 1911. She was assisted by her unmarried daughter Dorothy, who was the schoolmistress, whilst Mrs Wallington seems to have run the boarding establishment. The school was, however, neither large nor long-lived, with the last mention of it appearing in 'Gregory's Tiverton & District Directory' of 1919. Thereafter, Mrs Wallington continued to live at Morrells House for several years, but her daughter had moved away.

Morrell's, Lower Town: Mrs Wallington's home and school *Photo: Peter Bowers*

Mrs Edmonds' School

Mrs Ella Edmonds moved to Higher Town, Sampford Peverell in about 1925 to a house called Little Knowle. Although married, she was either widowed or estranged from her husband, and so lived there without a partner. She may have worked for a while as a school teacher, but there is no record of her having done so at the Sampford Peverell Church of England Primary School, and to have worked elsewhere would have involved some travelling. At some time between her arrival in the village and the 1940s, she started to teach children in her home, probably on an informal basis to begin with. Jan Barry, a resident of the village, attended her school in the 1940s when there were six pupils, mostly girls. She recalled that the school provided a quiet environment, where she was taught to read and write. Her recollection of Mrs Edmonds was that she was rather short, with a gentle, quiet manner of speaking. Lessons were for three or four hours in the morning, and in the afternoons Jan would often go for a walk in the countryside with her mother, and sometimes also with Mrs Edmonds. The school closed in 1947, when Mrs Edmonds died at the age of 74.

40 Higher Town: Mrs Edmonds' home and school
Photo: Peter Bowers

Tailpiece

The closure of Mrs Edmonds' school marked the end of private schooling in Sampford Peverell. The 1944 Education Act had introduced a second tier of education, such that children over the age of eleven were to be educated at grammar, secondary modern or technical schools. With no secondary school in the village, it became necessary for the older children to travel each day to and from Tiverton, or other nearby towns, to attend school. In a similar way, parents who wished that their younger children should be educated privately were now obliged to arrange transport for them to private schools in nearby towns and villages. However, private elementary schooling continued to be the choice for a minority of Sampford Peverell's children, with the majority attending the village Church of England Primary School.

Chapter VII

2000 onwards

From 2000 onwards there was no longer a statutory requirement for a log book to be maintained. This meant that the depth of detail and the delightful snippets of day-to-day happenings at the local school were no longer written up. In years to come this will no doubt be seen as a great loss.

Visit to Killerton, 2001 *Photo: Lynne Smith*

Education nationally has been subject to much political interference in recent years, with many new ideas implemented and then abandoned. The Department of Further Education and Schools has shown much enthusiasm for collaboration between schools. The Education Act 2002 introduced a number of measures, including the provision for a federation of schools, the aim of which was to bring schools together in a collaborative arrangement to raise standards, promote inclusion and find new ways of approaching teaching and learning. From September 2003 schools had the power to create a single, or joint, governing body across two or more of them to work together in this way.

Since the retirement of Michael Rumsey in 2000 Sampford Peverell School has had many changes of Head in a short period of time. In 2005 the school was put into 'Special Measures' after an inspection by OFSTED (the full title is Office for Standards in Education, Children's Services and Skills). However before the end of

Christmas play, 2005 *Photo: Lynne Smith*

the following year the school was again graded as 'satisfactory', and the governors decided in May 2010 to join the newly formed Children First Federation, which was to comprise the Primary schools of Sampford Peverell, Hemyock and Wilcombe in Tiverton. This meant that the school now had both a Head of Teaching and Learning and an Executive Head. However, the joining of the Federation had hardly been established when the government brought out a new act:

The Academies Act 2010

In the Queen's speech of 25 May 2010, legislation was announced enabling schools to achieve 'academy' status, providing greater management freedom. The Academies Bill was introduced into the House of Lords the following day and received Royal Assent on 27 July. The new academies' regime aims to give selected schools the opportunity to innovate and to raise standards by giving them greater freedom to control the way in which their affairs are managed. Academies are now given independence from local authority control; the freedom to set their own pay and conditions for staff; release from the National Curriculum; the freedom to set the lengths of the school day and term, and are given control of admissions (in compliance with existing law)[81].

---

[81] Thomson Snell and Passmore June 2011 at: www.ts-p.co.uk.

The Children First Federation (which now included Sampford Peverell School) joined the Primary Academy Trust in October 2011. This, as at March 2013, is an Academy Trust of eleven primary schools in Devon. An Academy Trust has to be a limited company which has charitable objectives. It has overall responsibility for the running of the academy and controls the land and other assets of the schools. The day-to-day management of the affairs of the Academy Trust is delegated to the Academy's governors (the local governors in the case of Sampford Peverell School) who run the Federation. This has led to the sharing of resources and staff, which can be beneficial to all, and standards have changed such that the 2012 Ofsted Inspection rated the school as 'Good across all five key areas of school life'. The Statutory Inspection of Anglican Schools (SIAS) report (the formal Church of England inspection) also found the school to be outstanding.

The precise future of the Sampford Peverell School in these early years of the twenty-first century is unclear. As this chapter has shown, major changes have occurred, and it sometimes appears that every new government administration feels the need to make yet more changes. We may hope, however, that the education provided in our small school will continue to provide our young people with the skills they will need to lead fulfilling lives.

River Dart residential visit, 2013

Appendix 1

Sources

Devon Heritage Centre:
Parish Registers of Baptisms, Marriages and Burials for Sampford Peverell, 1672-1956, ref. DRO 1198A/PR1-10

Vestry Minute Book for Sampford Peverell, 1841-1921, ref. DRO 1198A/PV1

Land Tax Assessment and Rate Book for Sampford Peverell, 1744-1840, ref. DRO 1198A-1/PC1-2

Tithe Map and Tithe Apportionment for Sampford Peverell, 1845, ref. DRO 1198A-2/PB1

Episcopal Visitations for Sampford Peverell

Shepherd's Academy inventory of contents

Letters by Earl Fortescue, Prebendary Brereton and the Head Master: The Devon County School, its objects, cost and studies. 1862.

Somerset Heritage Centre:
The Taunton Courier newspaper, various editions from 1810 to 1811.

Tiverton Museum of Mid Devon Life:
Tiverton Gazette newspaper, various editions 1858 to 1907

National Archives, Kew:
Files on the National School, Sampford Peverell NRA ref. ED103/86/33 and ED21/3786.

Websites:
www.britishnewspaperarchive.co.uk for The Western Times, Trewman's Exeter Flying Post and the Exeter and Plymouth Gazette. Numerous editions found by search engine.

www.ancestry.co.uk for censuses, parish registers, wills extracts and family trees

www.wikipedia.co.uk: various

Published works:

'Historical Notes on Devon Schools' by Robert Bovett, published by Devon County Council 1989.

'The Grand Western Canal' by Helen Harris, published by Devon Books 1996.

'Devon in the Religious Census of 1851' by Michael Wickes, published by M Wickes 1990.

'The English Peasantry' by Francis George Heath, published by F Warne & Co. 1874.

'A Village Childhood' by Denis Cluett, edited by Sampford Peverell Society, published by Charles Scott-Fox, 2007.

'Sampford Peverell: The Village, Church, Chapels and Rectories' by Sampford Peverell Society, published by Charles Scott-Fox, 2007.

Devon Trade Directories: White's 1850, 1878, 1890; Kelly's 1856, 1866, 1873, 1883, 1889, 1893, 1897, 1902, 1906, 1910, 1914, 1919, 1926, 1930, 1935, 1939 ; Billings' 1857; Morris' 1870; and Harrod's 1878.

Gregory's Tiverton & District Directory 1897, 1903, 1909, 1912, 1920 and 1923.

'The Short Titles Act 1896', section 2(1) and Schedule 2

'Education in Britain 1750–1914', W B Stephens, 1998, ISBN 0-333-60512-8

'Educational Documents, England and Wales 1816 to the present day', J Stuart MacLure, 1965, 1979, ISBN 0-416-72810-3 370.942

Collected reports and publications of the 'National Education League', Birmingham Central Library, A370.8, z1103222

'History and Mystery in Sampford Peverell' by Roger F S Thorne, published Ottery St Mary 1993.

Unpublished material:

Logbooks, Admissions Register and Punishment Book for Sampford Peverell National School (subsequently the Church of England Primary School)

'Sampford Peverell Church of England School 1874-1974' booklet.

Appendix 2

Head Teachers

Church of England Primary School

1850 - 1856	John Vickery
1865 - 1869	William Biddlecombe
1869 - 1870	Robert Jackson
1870 - 1871	Edwin Cook
1872 - 1872	William Lloyd
1872 - 1872	Jonathan Job
1875 - 1877	Robert Jackson
1877 - 1878	Thomas Lerwill
1878 - 1879	Walter Jewell
1880 - 1882	Charles Freeman
1882 - 1885	William Long
1886 - 1900	Isaac Bamforth
1900 - 1902	Henry Buckingham
1902 - 1930	John Henry Smith
1931 - 1949	Thomas Samuel
1949 - 1954	John Fawcett
1955 - 1955	Robert Mitchell
1955 - 1984	David Vickery
1984 - 1984	Simon Bartlett (A)
1985 - 2000	Michael Rumsey
2000 - 2001	Wendy Reynolds (A)
2002 - 2005	David Brown
2005 - 2007	Paul Walker
2007 - 2007	Joanna Rousseau
2008 - 2009	Janet Dinsmore
2009 - 2009	Gillian Kendrick (A)
2009 - 2014	Gillian Peters (B) (C)
2014 -	Lyn Brimson (B) (C)

A = Acting Head
B = Head of Teaching and Learning
C = The Executive Head is Jan Baker and the Chief Executive is Gary Chown

East Devon County School

1863 - 1866	Samuel Watson
1867 - 1879	Robert Clouting
1880 - 1883	Thomas Sandercock
1883 - 1886	John Hamilton Edmonds
1886 - 1907	William Goring Benge

Appendix 3

Standards of Education

These Standards applied in areas served by School Boards that had, after 1872, implemented by-laws mandating attendance until the age of 13. Children over the age of 10 were exempted if certified by the Inspector as satisfying the required standard of the Board concerned. The Standards required varied between a lower 4th Standard (for example in Birmingham) and the highest, the 6th Standard (as in Bolton). Also both the number of Standards, and the requirements for meeting them, changed over time.

The following are the six *Standards of Education* contained in the *Revised code of Regulations, 1872*

STANDARD I
Reading   One of the narratives next in order after monosyllables in an elementary reading book used in the school.
Writing   Copy in manuscript character a line of print, and write from dictation a few common words.
Arithmetic   Simple addition and subtraction of numbers of not more than four figures, and the multiplication table to multiplication by six.

STANDARD II
Reading   A short paragraph from an elementary reading book.
Writing   A sentence from the same book, slowly read once, and then dictated in single words.
Arithmetic   The multiplication table, and any simple rule as far as short division (inclusive).

STANDARD III
Reading   A short paragraph from a more advanced reading book.
Writing   A sentence slowly dictated once by a few words at a time, from the same book.
Arithmetic   Long division and compound rules (money).

STANDARD IV
Reading   A few lines of poetry or prose, at the choice of the inspector.
Writing   A sentence slowly dictated once, by a few words at a time, from a reading book, such as is used in the first class of the school.
Arithmetic   Compound rules (common weights and measures).

STANDARD V
Reading   A short ordinary paragraph in a newspaper, or other modern narrative.
Writing   Another short ordinary paragraph in a newspaper, or other modern narrative, slowly dictated once by a few words at a time.
Arithmetic   Practice and bills of parcels.

STANDARD VI
Reading   To read with fluency and expression.
Writing   A short theme or letter, or an easy paraphrase.
Arithmetic   Proportion and fractions (vulgar and decimal).

STANDARD VII
Standard VII was added in about 1900, as a response to raising the school leaving age.

Appendix 4

Attendance at The National School before 1900

The 1872 – 1900 Log Book gives some details of attendance at the school. Unfortunately, there are very few recorded numbers on roll, although there are many weekly attendance averages. These are interesting, because they show when the children were occupied with planting and harvesting and, of course, absent because of severe weather, epidemics and other illnesses and ailments. The outline findings are as follows.

1873 May 49 on roll.

1874 June (opening of the new school) to 1875 June. Average attendance for year 74.9

1876 Sept. Average for previous quarter 68.3

1880 March to 1881 March. Average annual attendance 73.8

1881 March to 1882 March. Average annual attendance 77.07

1883 Feb. Number on books 110. Weekly average 59.3!

1885 Jan. Number on books 118

1886 Jan. Average for previous quarter 75.9

1887 Jan. Average for quarter 76.3.

1889 Oct. Weekly average 109 'highest since school opened'.

1891 Sept. Free education started. Numbers rose to regularly more than 100.

1892 Jan. 122 on roll. A weekly average in May 117.5 'highest ever'.

1893 March 134 on roll.

1895 August '139 highest attendance ever.'

1897 May Weekly average 124.

During the 1890s attendance was regularly well over 100, except during the winter months November to March.

Appendix 5

Number of Pupils at the Church of England School 1873 - 2000

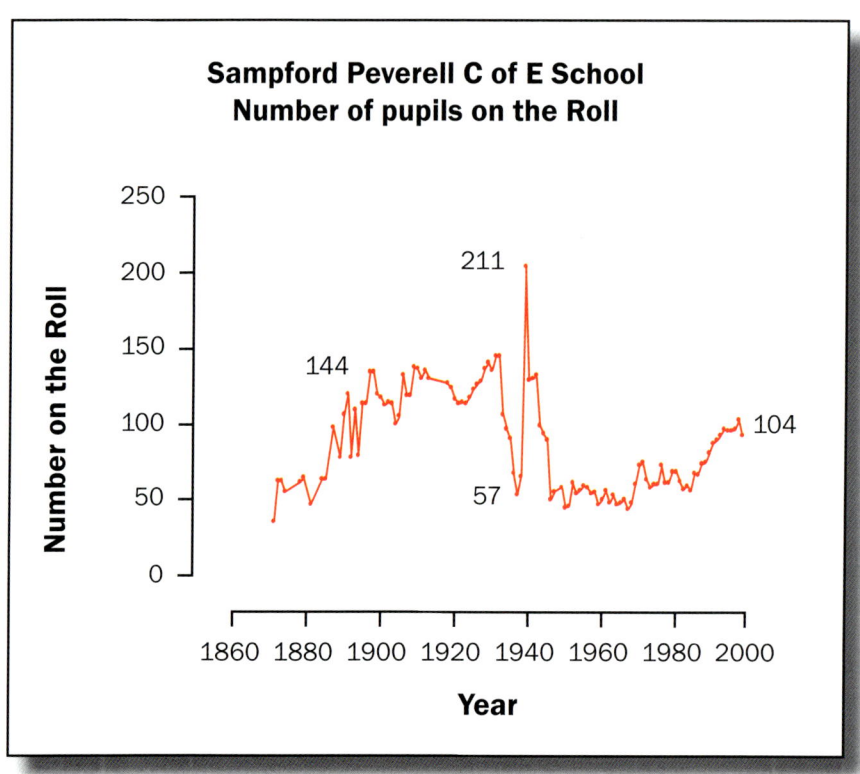

Note: The figures on the chart give the numbers of pupils enrolled in 1900 and in 2000, and also mark the highest and lowest numbers, in 1941 and 1939 respectively. The high point marks the influx of evacuee children. The sharp drop between 1934 (154 pupils) and 1939 (57 pupils) was, at least in part, due to several boys being moved from Sampford Peverell St. Boniface Home to another.

Information for the years before 1900 is of limited accuracy, as there are few records of numbers on the roll, but scattered references to weekly attendance numbers (see Appendix 4).

Appendix 6

Punishment Book for the Church of England School 1911 - 1984

Analysis of punishment by reason

disobedience	320
misconduct/misbehaviour	89
dishonesty/dishonest work	60
defacing/misuse of books, property	57
kicking/hitting/fighting	46
bullying	45
laziness	43
lying	43
impudence/impertinence	37
stealing	33
truancy/absconding	27
insolence	20
throwing stones etc.	19
talking/making a noise in class	18
carelessness	9
persistent lateness	9
cheating	8
defiance	7
not attending detention	7
swearing	7
indecent speech	6
playing in class time	6
trespassing on wrong playground	5
wasting material etc.	5
being disrespectful	4
absence through own fault	3
being obscene	3
persistent bad work	3
sulking	3
climbing on slates	1

Usually, the cane was the method of punishment used, the number of strokes varying from one to six. Most canings were given to boys.
Between 1931 and 1940 five girls were given the cane, administered on the hand. In the 1940s seven girls were caned for 'disorder in the cloakroom'.
The number of canings per year varied between twenty and forty-six from 1911 until 1937, but then tailed off to less than seventeen per year, with some years having no entries at all. The Punishment Book ends in 1984.

Index of Names

Acland, Sir Thomas Dyke	41, 45
Adams, William	9
Addington, Hon W W	41
Arnott, Dr Neil	18
Atkins, Miss	55
Badcock, John	15
Bailey, Miss	60
Baker, Jan	104
Balfour A J	53
Bamforth, Gertrude	27
Bamforth, Isaac	27, 29, 31, 32, 34, 36, 104
Bamforth, Mary	27
Bamforth, Maude	27
Barrie, Joseph	34
Barrons, Mr	29
Barry, Jan	98
Bartlett, Simon	104
Beadon, Mr	15
Beedell, John	17
Benge, Edith Hope (later Gilbert)	51
Benge, Mrs	49
Benge, William Goring	49-52, 104
Bennett, Edward	81
Bennett, Ronald	81
Bere, Revd Charles S	14, 38-41, 44-48
Biddlecombe, Mrs Eliza	20
Biddlecombe, William H	20, 22, 104
Bidgood, John	12, 13
Bond, Mrs	78
Bonnard, Mrs Jean	85
Boulton, Revd Dr Anthony	17, 19, 89
Bowden, Mr	32
Bradstrat, Miss	72
Bray, Miss	68
Brealy, Gordon	81
Brealy, Marion	81
Brereton, Revd Joseph Lloyd	37
Bridel, Mrs	85
Brimson, Lyn	104
Broom, Henry	17
Broomfield, Derrick	81
Broomfield, Molly	81
Broomfield, Roger	81
Brown, David	104
Brunskill, Revd Joseph G	70
Bryden, Mr R	35
Buckingham, Henry	28, 29, 56, 61, 104
Buller, General Sir Redvers Henry	50
Burgess, Mr	67
Burrough, John	45
Burrough, Mr and Mrs	18
Burston, Darrel	81
Burston, Wendy	81
Burton, Miss	72
Butler, Richard Austen	79
Candy, James	35
Carter, Miss Joan	85
Chappell, Marion	71
Chave, Elizabeth (later Merson)	3, 5
Chave, John	7, 10
Chave, John Richard	7, 8, 10-16, 37, 49, 96
Chave, Mary Taylor (later Lawrence)	7, 8
Chave, Mrs Eleanor	10-13
Chetham, Miss	79
Chown, Gary	104
Church, Col C B	85
Church, Mrs	85
Clapshaw, Mrs Rita	85
Clifford, John	53
Clouting, Mary	45, 46
Clouting, Reginald	45-47
Clouting, Robert	7, 45-47, 104
Cluett, Denis	56, 57
Coleman, Martin	81
Coleman, Miss	68
Coleridge, Samuel Taylor	41
Coleridge, Sir J T	41
Collard, Emma	32
Collingham, Lizzie	69
Connah, Mrs	79, 85
Cook, Edwin	104
Cowdell, Revd	53
Coyle, Revd M E	86
Creed, Mr	95
Cummins, Miss	67
Cure, Revd Edward Capel	32
Dinsmore, Janet	104
Disney, Colin	81
Disney, Jenifer	81
Dixon, Mrs	85
Drewe, E S	41
Druller, Edwin	1, 2
Dunn, Samuel	22, 28
Dunn, William	28
Ebrington, Viscount Hugh	37
Edmonds, John Hamilton	48, 104
Edmonds, Mrs Ella	97, 98
Elworthy, William	32
Evett, Phillip	81
Farr, Mrs Mary	25, 27, 28

Fawcett, John	104
Forster, William	21
Fortescue, 2nd Earl Hugh	37
Fortescue, 3rd Earl Hugh	37, 38, 40, 41, 46
Freeman, Charles	27, 36, 104
Froebel, Friedrich	30
Frost, Mr	31
Fry, Prior	95
Gilbert, Douglas Gerald	51
Gilbert, Edith Hope *(née Benge)*	51
Girdlestone, Revd Canon	42-44
Goffin, Jane	29
Goffin, Mary	81
Goffin, Mr C	85
Grant, Susan	81
Graves, Thomas	7
Graves-Morris, Dr J W	85
Hawkins, Rt Revd Richard	89
Haydon, Dr	35
Hayward, Lily	35
Hayward, Mr	14
Head, Mr R T	9
Hellier, Mary	32
Helmore, Frederick John	51
Hess, Susan	73
Hewett, Ann	6, 7
Hewett, James	6, 7, 17
Hill, Mrs	96
Holloway, Hetty	31
Holloway, Lily	31
Holloway, Mrs	31
Holly, Christine	81
Hookway (family)	73
Horne, Louise	5
Howard, Revd W	45
Howe, Graham	81
Hullah, John Pyke	31
Ireland, Revd George William Rossiter	14, 19, 21, 22, 25-28, 37
Jackson, Robert	27, 104
Jeffries, Margaret	71
Jennings, Samuel	2
Jewell, Walter	27, 29, 30, 104
Job, Jonathan	23, 25-27, 104
Keene, Sophia	5
Keitch, Mr K	85
Kendrick, Gillian	104
Kennaway, Sir John	41
Killingley, Louisa	7
King, Ann	81
King, David	81
Knight, Susannah	2
Kulczyk, Mr	85
Kulczyk, Mrs	85
Lake, William	53
Lawrence, Mary Taylor *(née Chave)*	7, 8
Lawrence, Samuel	3, 7-9, 11, 38
Lerwill, Thomas	27, 104
Lister, Mr D	85
Lister, Mrs	85, 86
Lloyd, Miss	67
Lloyd, William	22, 23, 104
Long, William	27, 30, 31, 104
Mainwaring, Sarah	5
Mardon, Mr J	96
Matthews, Mrs	85
Matthews, Paul	85
Maynard, Karen	81
Maynard, Vic	66
Membery, Jane	28
Mercer, Bishop Eric	85
Merson, Dr William Farrant	3-5
Merson, Elizabeth *(née Chave)*	3, 5
Merson, Maria *(née Morse)*	3, 4
Merson, Richard Chave	48, 49
Mitchell, Miss E D	85
Mitchell, Robert	104
Moon, Sheila	81
Morgan, Ada	25, 26
Morgan, Mrs	29
Morse, Amelia	6
Morse, Ann (junior)	6
Morse, Ann (senior)	4
Morse, James	5
Morse, Jane *(later Morton)*	1, 2, 4-6
Morse, Maria (junior)	3-5
Morse, Maria (senior) *(later Merson)*	3, 4
Morse, Salome	1, 2, 4-6
Morton, Amelia	4, 5
Morton, David	4
Morton, Jane (junior)	4, 5
Morton, Jane (senior) *(née Morse)*	1, 2, 4-6
Mowll, Mr A K	85
Mundella, Anthony	30
Nelson, Mrs	85
Nelson, Revd A B	85
Newton, Mrs	85
Norman, Florence	57
Norman, James John	38
Norrish, John	14
Palma, Mr	33

Palmerston, Lord	41
Pannell, Thomas Langford	2
Parker (family)	32
Parker, Eileen	73
Parkhouse, David	81
Parkhouse, Harriet	32
Parkhouse, Stephen	81
Partridge, William	9
Passmore, Glynis	81
Payne, Mr	6
Payne, William	17
Pedlar, Mr W F	7
Penkivil, Richard	17
Perkins, Alan	81
Perry, Mr H J	85
Peters, Gillian	104
Philpots, Bishop Henry	41
Pidsley, Revd Edward	16, 95
Pidsley, Revd Simon	2
Prescott, Master	81
Radford, Miss	28
Ramsey, Mr E	41
Redwood, Stuart	81
Rees, Revd John Jacob	60, 66, 67
Rendall, John King	28
Rendall, Mary Eleanor *(later Rossiter)*	28
Reynolds, Wendy	84, 90, 104
Richards, Nick	81
Robinson, Charlotte	38, 41
Robinson, John	38, 39, 41
Rogers, Miss E	85
Rossiter, Mary Eleanor *(née Rendall)*	28
Rossiter, Revd Philip C	22, 25, 27, 28, 32-34, 36, 54, 57, 60, 65
Rousseau, Joanna	104
Rowe, Brenda	81
Rumsey, Michael	88, 89, 91, 92, 99, 104
Russell, Dennis	66
Russell, Lisa	81
Salter, Joseph (junior)	31
Salter, Joseph (senior)	31
Sampson, Prebendary	85
Samuel, Mrs	57, 70
Samuel, Thomas John	57, 62, 66, 67, 70-72, 104
Sandercock, Mrs	47
Sandercock, Thomas J B	47, 48, 104
Saunders, Agnes	55, 56
Saunders, Janet	81
Scorse, Jack	60, 61, 64
Sellwood, Binford	48
Shackell, Richard	17
Sharland, David	81
Sharland, Denise	81
Sharland, Len	81
Sharland, Ruth	70, 71
Simpson, Miss	72
Skinner, Richard	17
Smith, John Henry	26, 55-59, 61, 63, 64, 104
Smith, Mary	55, 64
Smith, Wilfred	55
Smith, Winifred	55
Snell, Mr	14
Spens, Sir William	79
Stone, David	81
Sully, William	31, 32
Surridge, John	17
Tapp, Miss	55
Taylor, Francis (junior)	95
Thomas, Miss	96
Troyte, Major	41, 47
Tucker, Miss	56
Turner, Christine	81
Turner, Francis	81
Veale, Revd	53
Venner, Ron	96
Vickary *(or Vickery)*, John	20, 104
Vickery, Caroline	81
Vickery, David	79, 81, 82, 85, 104
Vickery, Dawn	81
Vickery, Mrs	85
Voaden, Percy James	57, 60, 63
Walker, Paul	104
Wallington, Miss Dorothy	97
Wallington, Mrs Bright	97
Watson, Samuel William	39, 41, 44, 45, 104
Webber, Jane	38
West, Miss	60
White, Harry	32
White, Mr	32
White, Stephen	81
Williams, Audrey	81
Williams, John	38
Wilmet, Edward	45
Wilson-Smith, Gerry	85
Wood, A E	85
Wood, Mr	62
Workman, Roger	81
Wright, David	81
Wright, Ken	85
Wright, Sylvia	81
Young, Captain	64